GOING BIG

GOING
BIG

FDR's Legacy,
Biden's New Deal,
and the Struggle to Save Democracy

ROBERT KUTTNER

THE
NEW
PRESS

NEW YORK
LONDON

© 2022 by Robert Kuttner
Foreword © 2022 by Joseph E. Stiglitz
All rights reserved.
No part of this book may be reproduced, in any form, without written permission from the publisher.

Requests for permission to reproduce selections from this book should be made through our website: https://thenewpress.com/contact.

Published in the United States by The New Press, New York, 2022

Distributed by Two Rivers Distribution

ISBN 978-1-62097-727-9 (hc)
ISBN 978-1-62097-728-6 (ebook)

CIP data is available

The New Press publishes books that promote and enrich public discussion and understanding of the issues vital to our democracy and to a more equitable world. These books are made possible by the enthusiasm of our readers; the support of a committed group of donors, large and small; the collaboration of our many partners in the independent media and the not-for-profit sector; booksellers, who often hand-sell New Press books; librarians; and above all by our authors.

www.thenewpress.com

Composition by dix!
This book was set in Garamond Premier Pro

Printed in the United States of America

10 9 8 7 6 5 4 3 2 1

For Joan, again

Contents

Foreword

Joseph E. Stiglitz

The United States, and the world, are at a fork. Somehow, we managed our way through the presidency of Donald Trump, with all his divisiveness and mendacity, and, as this book goes to press, through the worse pandemic and deepest downturn in memory. As Robert Kuttner points out forcefully in this book, there is the real possibility that President Biden will restore the progressive agenda, with all the idealism upon which it is based. It is a *great transformation*, one the country and the world badly need, as we face unprecedented challenges of inequality, climate change, and structural change—moving from a manufacturing economy to a service-based knowledge economy. And yet we also might plunge into an abyss of repression.

As his touchstone, and Biden's, Kuttner appropriately invokes FDR. President Franklin Delano Roosevelt presided over a grand transformation almost a hundred years ago, as we moved from an agrarian and rural economy to an urban manufacturing one—and reversed the ravages of laissez-faire that marked the Roaring Twenties as well as the Gilded Age of an earlier generation. Key parts of his legacy, such as Social Security, have become central parts of our social fabric, but other parts, such as the rebalancing of the power of workers and the taming of finance, have been eviscerated, and especially so during the four decades beginning with Carter and Reagan, during which neoliberalism, the belief that markets on their own would solve society's problems, reigned supreme. But as Kuttner rightly warns, the country could take the other fork—a victory for the forces of reaction in every sphere of our society.

It's a familiar story. This country was founded with a split personality, a commitment to freedom and equality—"All men are created equal"—resting on a bedrock of slavery. The standard narrative is that with each trauma, we emerged stronger than before. But each time, many of the advances that we made in the years immediately after the trauma were reversed in the years following: the short period of Reconstruction was followed by Jim Crow. In this century, the advances in civil rights in the 1960s, including on voting, have been at least partially undone—and the Republican Party is making concerted effort to undermine these advances even more. Moreover, the fact that progressives fended off these attacks in the past is no assurance that they will prevail now: today's battleground is different.

In this foreword, I want to put some perspective on what's at stake, what the battle is all about. We all know the skirmishes, from abortion to voting rights to unionization to curbing the power of finance and monopolies. Behind it all is a view of a Good Society, the nature of the individual, the relationship of the individual to society, and the role of markets in all of this.

I approach these issues partially from the lens of an economist: since the beginning of capitalism, there have been two views on the origins of inequality and the sources of growth—what gives rise to "the wealth of nations."

One strand focuses on rugged individualism, competition, emphasizing the central role of markets and entrepreneurship. In this perspective, greed is good—the pursuit of self-interest leads to the well-being of society. As Adam Smith, the father of modern economics, put it, "It is not from the benevolence of the butcher, the brewer, or the baker that we expect our dinner, but from their regard to their own interest." It followed, in these theories, that differences in incomes were the "just deserts"—those who contributed more to society were correspondingly rewarded. These are the views of Smith that the right has championed.

The other view, more consistent with perspectives growing out of the Enlightenment (of which Adam Smith was one of the important thinkers), was that the wealth of nations grows out of advances in science and in mechanisms of social organization—allowing larger groups of people to cooperate. It is these "enlightenment advances" that explain why our standards of living today are so much higher than they were just 250 years ago; why, after standards of living had stagnated for centuries after centuries, they finally began to soar. *Collective action* is central, and there is more to collective action and cooperation than that coordinated through the marketplace via the price system. Even a simple society needs rules and regulations—the Ten Commandments being an example. But rules and regulations are even more imperative in a complex twenty-first-century society where externalities—created when the market produces too much of things that harm others and too little of those things that benefit others—have taken on first-order importance. The climate crisis is the result of firms and individuals producing excessive greenhouse gas emissions; the current pandemic has been aggravated by those selfishly refusing to wear masks, practice social distancing, and get vaccinated—not thinking at all of the risks they are imposing on the rest of society.

At the core of success in a modern economy are *public goods*, from which all benefit—in particular, advances in basic science—and markets will never invest sufficiently in those things from which everyone benefits. Indeed, had we not had the public-supported advances in biology leading to our understanding of mRNA vaccines, the pandemic would have been far worse. In short, the whole is greater than the sum of its parts.

Thus, a central tenet of modern economics is that unfettered markets cannot be relied upon, for a whole variety of reasons. Among those reasons is that markets are far less benign, even within the limited domain in which they might work, than the above quotation from Smith would suggest. Markets are typically not competitive. There are a host of ways by which some can take advantage of others, exploiting them one way or another, whether through physical force—sometimes condoned or implemented by the state, as in slavery—or simply acting on human vulnerabilities or asymmetries, in either information (where one party to a transaction knows more than the other) or market power. This interpretation of economic relations emphasizes inequalities arising not from "just deserts" but from one form or another of exploitation.

Despite the popular caricature of his teachings, Adam Smith had a more balanced understanding than his latter-day followers. Smith understood that the world is complex, and in his writings, he reflected on both of the perspectives I've described. He recognized that markets only worked to advance the interests of society if there was competition. But he recognized that that was not the natural state of the economy: "People of the same trade seldom meet together, even for merriment and diversion, but the conversation ends in a conspiracy against the public, or in some contrivance to raise prices." He recognized too the dangers of an unregulated marketplace and the disadvantageous position of workers:

> Masters are always and everywhere in a sort of tacit, but constant and uniform, combination, not to raise the wages of labour above their actual rate. . . . Masters, too, sometimes enter into particular combinations to sink the wages of labour even below this rate. These are always conducted with the utmost silence and secrecy.

It followed that "when the regulation, therefore, is in support of the workman, it is always just and equitable; but it is sometimes otherwise when in favour of the masters."

FDR became president well before modern economics clarified our understanding of the strengths and limits of markets. But in the midst of the Great Depression, you didn't need the mathematical models at the core of these later advances to realize that the economy wasn't working well, that people were suffering, and that there were grave inequities. Many of the solutions that FDR proposed were just common sense—to redress the imbalances of power between workers and employers, workers should have the right to unionize. Markets had failed to provide for a secure retirement or deal with the risk of disability—and in Europe, it had already been well demonstrated that government could remedy these deficiencies. The Great Depression was in part a result of excesses in the financial market—forms of "greed," self-interest that did not serve the well-being of society—and FDR understood that government regulations should and could curb such excesses.

In other areas, FDR's actions were limited by the understandings of the time: he grasped that expansionary spending (the New Deal) would stimulate the economy—and it did—but he worried about the resulting debt and the subsequent faltering commitment to expansionary fiscal policy.

While in some ways World War II interrupted the "revolution" of recreating an economy that was more stable and better served society, in two critical aspects it furthered this progressive agenda: First, to win the war, we, through government, had to invest enormously in science and technology—what I have argued is the root of the source of the wealth of nations. Thus government support of research became one of the pillars of our growth in succeeding decades. The second way the war furthered the progressive agenda was the hidden "industrial policy"—policies in which government played a central role in reshaping the economy. The war necessitated moving individuals from the rural areas to the cities and retraining them for a modern manufacturing economy; the GI bill provided the advanced education that a modern twentieth-century economy needed.

Joe Biden seems to understand this legacy, and he hopes to build on it. Markets on their own are not very good in making such structural transformations—for instance, those in the declining sectors typically don't have the resources to make the necessary investments to make themselves more productive in the ascending sectors. One interpretation of the Great Depression is precisely that it reflected the limitations of the market in making a smooth transition from agriculture to manufacturing.

As Kuttner points out, with the end of the war the progressive agenda continued, at least for a generation: even under a Republican president, Eisenhower, the federal government took on broadened responsibilities, with national infrastructure, education, and research programs. The war had further exposed the inequities of race, as African Americans fought and died for a country that refused to treat them as full citizens. And the fight over civil rights in the 1960s, of which I was proud to be a part, showed the depths of two strands that had long existed in America: the passion on the part of some for social justice, and the deep racism of a significant part of the country. Martin Luther King Jr., most forcefully, made the link between economic, racial, and social justice in the United States. Globally, the UN Declaration of Human Rights began the process of establishing a set of norms for what constituted a decent society. Even with access to health care increasingly recognized as a basic human right, politics in America prevented the country from doing what the UK and other European countries did, in spite of being at the time clearly the richest country in the world—though at least under Johnson we provided health care to the aged.

The economic and social solidarity of the war helped bring about the country's period of greatest prosperity (as measured by the rate of growth of GDP), and though it was not fully shared—discrimination continued—it was an era of *more* shared prosperity, with gaps between the rich and poor markedly decreased.

But all of this progress in the progressive agenda came to a halt, as Kuttner points out, beginning, ironically with a Democratic president, Jimmy Carter. He didn't use the Clintonesque word "triangulation," but that's what he engaged in: he thought that by making the Democratic Party more like the Republican Party, by advocating what were called market-friendly policies, such as deregulation, he could enhance the party's electoral success.

Behind this was both a battle of ideas and a battle of interests. The latter was obvious: business interests—particularly important in financing increasingly expensive electoral campaigns—had long bridled at the attempts, beginning with FDR, to tame and temper the market, to make it better serve the interests of society. By the 1970s, they were again politically ascendant.

I was part of the battle of ideas. To me, it was a cruel irony that just as economists had rigorously established the limitations of markets, had provided solid foundations for why regulations were needed, and even had begun the analyses of how to better regulate the market, our political leaders began espousing ideas that went in exactly the opposite direction. While my research and that of others had shown that stock market value maximization would not lead to societal well-being, Milton Friedman, as a polemist par excellence, argued the opposite—and his ideological stance fit well with the era of Reagan, Thatcher, and Pinochet.

Neoliberalism—the belief that unfettered markets were

efficient and stable and should be at the center of our economy and society—ignored these advances in modern economics and forgot the lessons of history, including that of the Great Depression, and we have paid a high price. The Depression should have taught us that markets are *not* stable and efficient—high levels of unemployment could persist for a very long time. We should not have had to have the Great Recession to relearn the lesson. Keynes taught us that fiscal policy can be very effective in rejuvenating an economy in a slump. We should not have had to watch the anemic recovery from the Great Recession, the result of too little fiscal policy and too much reliance on monetary policy, to have relearned that lesson.

The simplistic neoliberal ideology, which triumphed in both parties—with a more humanitarian touch in the Democratic Party—held that downsizing government, including deregulation, privatization, and outsourcing government activities to the private sector, would lead to greater prosperity, and through a mystical process called trickle-down economics, all would benefit. Some half-century later, we should declare: this neoliberal experiment has been a failure, with lower growth and the benefits of that limited growth going overwhelmingly to those at the top. I remember the pride that came with the reduction in the numbers of federal government employees. Our metrics did not allow us to ascertain whether that corresponded to an increase in the well-being of ordinary citizens. We now know that this was an era in which large swaths of Americans were *not* doing well.

In spite of its failures, the era of neoliberalism is far from over. It has infected the way too many political leaders and many citizens see the economic choices we face. And it has left a political legacy evident in Covid—a resistance to regulations that would clearly enhance public health and societal well-being, a lack of trust in government, in our institutions, in each other, a lack of cooperation, an undermining of respect for science and truth, all core Enlightenment values. All of this is a threat to the continuation of progress—it undermines what I have argued is at the heart of our success in raising living standards for the past two and a half centuries. Indeed, it undermines our ability even to work together as a society.

This is where Joe Biden steps into the scene: at last, we have the possibility of restoring the progressive agenda. The politics are right: having seen the dark side of the alternative in the form of President Trump, having seen how the Republican Party has responded to the defeat of Trump with a renewed vigor in undermining democracy, there is real urgency in presenting a convincing case for an alternative. The timing is right: the country and the world are facing a multitude of crises, from the pandemic to climate change to the health crisis, in an era where authoritarianism rules once again over a majority of citizens around the world. Only the progressive agenda holds out prospects for making significant inroads in addressing these crises. It has shown creativity in coming up with new solutions to long-standing problems, such as the public option, not just for health care, but for housing and retirement, enhancing competition and innovation.

Unlike the conservative agenda, which hankers after a world gone by, and tries to shoehorn today's problems into past "solutions," the progressive agenda understands that the world is always evolving, and therefore our solutions—the policies we need to address today's problems—need to be ever evolving. Twenty-first-century competition policy is of necessity different from what might have worked at the end of the nineteenth. The viral spread of mis- and disinformation over social media was simply not a problem confronting the world of the past, but it is one that we have to address today.

Most Americans strongly support most elements of this progressive agenda—and among our young people, to whom the future of the country belongs, the support is overwhelming. A twenty-first-century government has to go beyond social protection and maintaining full employment. Regulations have to be adapted, research is of ever-increasing importance, and making our cities, in which an increasing fraction of our citizens live, more livable is an imperative. There needs to be lifelong investment in people—what some call the caring economy—beginning with childcare and preschool but extending to college and on-the-job training, health care, and care for our aged.

This broadened vision of what needs to be done needs to be accompanied, as I have suggested, with a broadened vision of how it should be done, not just the public options to which I referred earlier, but a wider array of institutional arrangements, with greater emphasis on cooperatives, NGOs, and so on—a richer ecology of institutions than just governments and markets. But we can't lose sight that we, collectively, through government, set the rules of the game, that the rules of the game matter, and that they have to be set in a way that advances the interests of all citizens, including those who have historically been marginalized.

So we are at a fateful fork in the road. We could—and I strongly believe—should go down the one I've just described. But it is far from inevitable. There is a political war going on, with one side engaging in voter suppression and a campaign of mis- and disinformation. The progressive side can't match the tactics—that would be self-defeating. It has to win by engendering engagement, through an understanding of where we are, how we got here, and what the stakes are. Kuttner's book makes all of this crystal clear.

GOING BIG

1

The Improbable Progressive

Joe Biden's presidency will be either a historic pivot back to New Deal economics and forward to energized democracy, or a heartbreaking interregnum between two bouts of deepening American fascism. We are facing the most momentous threat to the American republic since the Civil War.

The illusion of a middle ground has evaporated. Democrats looking for someone to meet halfway have scarcely any Republican takers. The Trump ideology includes not only racialized nationalism, but a systematic scheme to cling to power by destroying democracy at every level of government. Republicans are increasingly condoning violence and vigilantism on the part of extremists in their base, who include several members of Congress. Our corporate center right has made a pact with the devil, in which Republicans defend low taxes, deregulation, destruction of labor rights, and extreme economic concentration, and much of the financial elite turns a blind eye to the destruction of democracy—even welcomes it.

Throughout the West, the far right has gained ground. But only in America has it captured one of the two major governing parties. This way lies something very much like fascism.

Standing in the way of this grim future is seventy-nine-year-old Joe Biden and a wafer-thin majority in Congress. As this book goes to press in January 2022, much of Biden's bold agenda has been blocked in the Senate by Republicans and two corporate

Democrats. This blockage has intensified a downward spiral of lost public confidence, media scorn, declining approval ratings, and predictions of electoral disaster in November. But presidents have come back from worse, and the stakes are immense. If Democrats lose Congress, Republican autocracy only increases, setting the stage for Trumpism's return and the end of democracy.

This book argues that the Democrats can succeed—and have to succeed; and that Biden was right to think big. It is a fantasy to imagine that thinking small would have produced a better bulwark against Trumpism, much less addressed the cumulative ills that in turn led to Trump. Going small would have produced a slower economic recovery. It would neither have kept the pandemic at bay nor fixed the supply chain debacle. Conciliatory moderation would not have led Republics to reciprocate; it would have been taken as a sign of weakness and invited even more far-right ferocity. A mere return to economic "normal" would have condemned most Americans to declining economic horizons, more frustration, and more support for demagogues. Biden's return to the New Deal was long overdue.

The book will review the greatness of the New Deal as a model for progressive policy and politics, as well as the dynamics of its steady reversal—in which Democratic presidents were complicit. We will explore how Biden found his way back to FDR, the multiple obstacles to his success, and the dire consequences of failure.

Between March 2020 and the summer of 2021, Joe Biden was the luckiest politician in living memory. After his feckless campaign for the Democratic nomination nearly collapsed in February, Biden gained a big win in the southern primaries, notably South Carolina, in March. Those wins created a bandwagon effect, and he quickly became the de facto nominee. Given the immense stakes of ousting Trump, Biden benefited from rare Democratic party unity, even from activists well to his left who had supported

Elizabeth Warren or Bernie Sanders. More remarkably, surprise victories in two Georgia Senate races delivered Biden a bare majority in both houses of Congress. Thanks to Trump's overreach and the loyalty to the republic of a few key Republicans, a coup was blocked and Biden was able to take office.

Progressives like me were grateful for the ouster of Trump, but we had few illusions about Joe Biden. Given his history, we expected that he would govern as the third centrist Democratic president in a row, not unlike Hillary Clinton had she been elected. That would have continued a toxic syndrome in which socially liberal Democrats are economically allied with Wall Street and fail to deliver for a disaffected and disrespected working class—who become easy prey for the likes of Trump.

But Biden surprised us all by resolving to govern in the spirit of FDR. His program of public investments and social supports was the boldest since Roosevelt. Better yet, it delivered concrete benefits to the very people who had been deserting Democrats for decades. The benefits were direct and easy to grasp. Biden was able to use the annual budget reconciliation process, which cannot be filibustered in the Senate, to enact the March 2021 emergency legislation titled the American Recovery Plan Act (ARPA), which passed 219–212 in the House and 50–49 in the Senate, on straight party-line votes. Thanks to the $1.9 trillion package, the recession was abbreviated, suffering was reduced, and the economy ended 2021 with record growth and low unemployment.

Among its many accomplishments, ARPA provided $300 a month in extended unemployment compensation, direct payments of $1,400 to families, and a refundable child tax credit that really amounts to a universal basic income for families with children. The government sends parents of children monthly checks of $250 per child between the ages of six and seventeen, and $300 for kids under six. This basic income supplement, which is automatic and not means tested, cuts the child poverty rate in half. In addition, the law provided $350 billion to hard-pressed state and local governments so that the recession would not be compounded by layoffs, $130 billion for public schools, and almost $40 billion for colleges and universities. All of this was intended to help offset the economic damage and personal hardship of Covid. The law also provided upwards of $150 billion to defeat the pandemic, including $50 billion to underwrite vaccinations and another $48 billion for testing and contact tracing. Since all of this practical outlay goes to red states as well as blue ones, in normal times this legislation might have attracted some Republican support. But it received not a single Republican vote.

Thanks to ARPA, the poverty rate declined during a deep recession, something that had never happened before. Child poverty fell by almost half. Biden did not succeed in raising the minimum wage, but the income supports and the robust recovery gave workers rare bargaining power to hold out for terms well above the minimum wage. A week after signing ARPA on March 11, Biden met with a group of presidential historians at the White House and resolved to go even bigger.

Equally superb were Biden's appointments and his revision of the economic conventional wisdom about everything from budget balance to free trade. More than any president since FDR, Biden has embraced labor unions. His support for extensive industrial policies to rebuild American manufacturing and mitigate climate change evokes Roosevelt's national mobilization during World War II.

The idea of governing like Roosevelt with a working majority of three in the House and zero in the Senate was as risky as it was audacious. But I will argue that reclaiming FDR's legacy was and is exactly what the country needs.

Biden's luck held through the summer of 2021. The pandemic was winding down; the recovery was gathering force; he made no unforced political errors; party unity continued in Senate confirmation of key appointees, who were the most progressive lot since FDR. Biden's approval ratings in the polls were far from stratospheric. Some 40 percent of Americans were Trumpers no matter what Biden delivered, but his ratings were more than serviceable. Voters approved of Biden by a margin of about fifteen points overall from February through June. An even higher percentage liked specific elements of his program.

And then Lady Luck deserted Biden. Though his administration was handling the pandemic far better than Trump had, Covid had its own rhythms. In a fourth wave beginning in late July, cases started surging and the promised economic reopening had to be deferred, leaving voters—parents, workers, and ordinary people needing a respite—frustrated and cranky. A supply-chain crisis several decades in the making spiked consumer price inflation. In August, Biden's resolve to end America's interminable entanglement in Afghanistan produced a messy final exit. Historians will long debate whether any exit could have been executed more cleanly. In fact, voters supported the decision to leave Afghanistan by a margin of 73 to 27. But the images of people desperate to get out and government forces being routed cost Biden dearly.

Democrats who had been uncharacteristically united in the spring then indulged their differences in the fall. A small splinter of corporate Democrats in the House blocked Biden's full program. By the time a compromise delivered part of Biden's infrastructure bill, Election Day was long past and Democrats paid the political price. Biden looked weak and inept. This stalemate cost Democrats the governorship of Virginia, as well as many state and local legislative seats that were up on the off-off-year election, and the enthusiasm of voters.

By Labor Day, Biden's approval ratings were negative and steadily worsening. By November, voters disapproved of his performance by as much twenty points, though his popularity began to rebound once Congress finally acted on his program.

Some have argued that Biden overreached, and that it's time for him to repair to the center. Even the *New York Times*, which had strongly supported Biden's program, published a perverse editorial after the November election defeats, titled "Democrats, Get Real." According to the Times editorial board, "Tuesday's results are a sign that significant parts of the electorate are feeling leery of a sharp leftward push in the party." The editorial also contended that the Democrats suffered election losses because "the party has become distracted from crucial issues like the economy, inflation, ending the coronavirus pandemic and restoring normalcy in schools and isn't offering moderate, unifying solutions to them," and called on Biden to embrace bipartisanship.

That logic, which echoes and reinforces the conventional wisdom, is backward. What cost the Democrats last November was not their leftism but the spectacle of a governing party that looked like it couldn't govern. Biden was plenty popular after enactment of his first New Deal–scale program, ARPA, in March. The elements of his bolder programs of infrastructure investments and social supports are immensely popular as well.

With minor exceptions, there is little bipartisanship to be had. Biden could move toward the center or even the center right, and that would not produce more Republican support in the Senate, where the Republican playbook is to undermine the Biden presidency no matter what he proposes and to destroy American democracy along with it. The thirteen House Republicans who did vote for the "bipartisan" stripped-down infrastructure bill that passed in November were vilified as traitors by their colleagues. Several are not running for reelection.

Most importantly, America urgently needs the kind of New Deal that Biden is promoting. Corporate concentration has reached a peak not seen since the Gilded Age, with the result that all of the economy's net gains go to billionaires and most working families are earning less in real terms than a generation ago. Intensified corporate use of outsourcing and contract work has deprived tens of millions of Americans of decent jobs and earnings. Decades of disinvestment in basic public infrastructure have left the country with outmoded basic systems of water, electric power, and public transportation and woefully unprepared for the added investments to protect against the ravages of climate change and to move to renewable energy. The loss of basic manufacturing has cost America both jobs and regional activity, as well a heavy reliance on China for supply chains. The supply chain fiasco, in turn, caused bottlenecks and inflation.

Biden's original ten-year infrastructure plan addressed long-neglected public needs. It included $556 billion to invest in U.S. manufacturing and supply chains; $387 billion for schools and other public buildings; $100 billion for broadband; $111 billion for water infrastructure; $151 billion for rail and public transit; $82 billion to modernize power grids; $363 billion in clean energy subsidies and tax credits; $157 billion for electric vehicles; $154 billion for roads and bridges; $42 billion for ports and airports. These are ten-year totals. By the time Congress belatedly pass the much-diminished compromise that Biden signed on November 14, the total had been slashed to $550 billion in new spending over ten years. The funds for manufacturing and clean energy were eliminated entirely. The package did keep funding for urgently needed public investments such as water and power infrastructure, rail and mass transit, though at reduced levels. Republican legislators will take credit for these in ribbon-cutting ceremonies in their districts, even though most voted against it.

The pandemic revealed the stresses on working families in a country that lacks social supports that are universal in much of the West—comprehensive and universal health coverage; publicly sponsored and subsidized pre-kindergarten and childcare;

decent and well-compensated nursing and home care; free or affordable higher education with no student debt; paid family and medical leave. Biden's program made a start on providing these supports to all families. These are the kinds of programs that are politically hard to enact—and broadly popular once enacted.

At its original scale of $3.5 trillion over a decade, Biden's Build Back Better program was a down-payment on the social investments that America has needed for decades, and the even larger investments in climate resilience we will need going forward. Its particulars propose the most imaginative uses of public policy and public investment since Roosevelt. With unrelenting Republican opposition and the intransigence of Democrats Joe Manchin and Kyrsten Sinema, Biden had to settle for less. But these programs serve ordinary Americans and are good politics once enacted. It would be a travesty to conclude that Biden dreamed too big.

As approved by the House on November 9, the bill extended the near-universal child tax credit for a year (after which it will be hard to repeal). The bill provided $150 billion for better home health care, both for the frontline care workers and for people who need it. It also provided half a trillion dollars for clean energy, including $144 billion for renewable electricity, and additional funding for electric vehicles and public transportation. At a time of scarce affordable housing and waiting lists for vouchers and public housing, the measure provided over $100 billion for housing assistance. Even with the deeper cuts demanded by Joe Manchin as a condition of enactment by the Senate, it is the most impressive expansion of basic social insurance since Lyndon Johnson's Great Society.

With the 20-20 wisdom of hindsight, one can fault Biden tactically, for failing to make an earlier deal with Manchin for a smaller Build Back Better. But Biden had progressives in Congress to contend with. And Manchin, with personal interests in coal, was also demanding that Biden scrap of much of the climate agenda. These Monday morning quarterback criticisms also excuse Republicans, especially supposed moderates like Senators Mitt Romney, Susan Collins, and Lisa Murkowski. If even one of these worked with Biden, Manchin's opposition would be far less potent. Biden's tactical flaws pale compared to Republican evils in wanting to ignore urgent needs entirely and kill our democracy.

To fully understand the risks and opportunities of this fraught moment, we need to take a deeper look at the past. The New Deal was revolutionary. But even at the peak moment of the disgrace of laissez-faire capitalism, Roosevelt's New Dealers did not get everything they wanted or needed. In a market economy where most ownership remained private, financial capitalism retained immense economic and political power to undermine Roosevelt's efforts. It took only the right combination of circumstances beginning in the 1970s for predatory capital to get loose once again and repeat the excesses of the 1920s, and then some.

In the half-century since Lyndon Johnson's Great Society, financial and corporate capitalists shook off the restraints of the New Deal. They invented new abuses that produced grotesque inequality and eventually crashed the economy. Worse, this reversion to the brutality of raw capitalism was abetted by three consecutive Democratic presidents.

Jimmy Carter, before Ronald Reagan, promoted deregulation and "supply side" tax-cutting to reward the wealthy. He attacked government. Despite a huge post-Watergate legislative majority, he did little for the labor movement. Carter was a good-government "process liberal," but substantively the most conservative Democratic president since Grover Cleveland.

Bill Clinton joined the chorus declaring that government was the problem, not the solution. He scapegoated people reliant on welfare. On the advice of Robert Rubin and Lawrence Summers, Clinton made a political and financial alliance with Wall Street and promoted new forms of deregulation that enabled new abuses. Clinton also made budget balance the holy grail of economy policy. The next Democrat, Barack Obama, retained many of Clinton's advisers and fiscal ideology.

When the accumulated excesses of deregulated financial capitalism finally crashed the economy in the fall of 2008 on the watch of George W. Bush, Obama missed his Roosevelt moment. He and his team, mostly Clinton alums, propped up the big predatory banks rather than breaking them up. Obama made budget balance the centerpiece of his economic program in early 2010, long before the economy was close to full recovery. He was more concerned with deficits than with public investment and job creation.

Under all these Democratic presidents, the economic situation of ordinary Americans steadily worsened. The result of the alliance of Democratic presidents with Wall Street was to distance the party of the common people from its natural constituency of working families. It was only a matter of time before we got the faux-populism and neo-fascism of someone like Donald Trump.

Even Roosevelt's New Deal had to make terrible compromises with racist legislators to win enactment of his program. Biden, to achieve the necessary governing majority, needs to achieve durable multiracial coalitions—where both FDR and LBJ failed. Roosevelt had to conquer fascism in Europe. Biden must defeat it at home.

History can be grossly unjust. Bill Clinton and Barack Obama took the Democratic Party deeper into the neoliberal wilderness, obsessing about budget balance, making alliances with Wall Street, and driving working-class voters into the arms of the Tea Parties and then Trump. Yet both were reelected; and by conventional measures both had successful presidencies.

Biden took office at the pit of a pandemic and an associated recession. He ventured an admirable recovery program and began to reclaim the New Deal legacy that had been an epic political success as well as beneficial to countless ordinary Americans. Yet it is Biden who seems on the brink of failure, not because of his own deficiencies or misjudgments but because the results of so many bad long-term policies and political failures by his Democratic predecessors exploded during his presidency.

Here is the great paradox of this fraught political moment. Biden is being pilloried for attempting too much. But if anything, Biden's vision needs to be even more radical. Beyond the welcome and long-overdue public investment, a deeper challenge is to radically reform predatory capitalism. A second urgent need is to finally overcome the legacy of white supremacy, which time after time has destroyed the broad class coalitions needed for durable progressivism. A third challenge is to redefine America's role in the world, especially but not exclusively on climate change. Without extraordinary measures and American leadership on climate, Biden could do everything else right, and escalating climate disasters could destroy economic prospects, discredit government, and bring more dictators to power.

To avoid repudiation by the voters, Biden will need the kind of luck that shined on him in 2020 and the first half of 2021— and more. It is not hard to tell a story of impending disaster in the 2022 midterms. Biden's approval ratings continue to languish. Inflation doesn't subside. The pandemic doesn't quite end. The stripped-down Build Back Better program, though still impressive, takes too long to make a dramatic difference in people's lives. Resurgent Republicans are on the march while dispirited Democrats stay home.

I choose to tell a more hopeful story. But events will have to break right for Biden, as they did during the election and his first six months as president. Voters appalled by Trump and an increasingly unhinged Republican Party will need to remember why they turned out at record levels in 2018 and 2022. There will need to be even greater turnout in 2022 to create a mobilization that provides a sufficient buffer against escalating voter suppression. This outcome is far from assured—but it is definitely possible and urgently necessary.

Why did Joe Biden, ostensibly the most centrist of Democrats in the 2020 field, turn out to be the most progressive Democratic president since Franklin Roosevelt? Unless one looked carefully and selectively, there was little in Biden's prior history as a senator and vice president to suggest that he would be notably different from the three centrist Democratic presidents who preceded him. One can think of several examples of leaders who became emboldened in mid-career as a result of circumstances. Lincoln went from cautious opponent of slavery in the territories to Great Emancipator. Both Roosevelts turned out to be far more progressive as presidents than their early histories suggested. But Lincoln was fifty-two when he became president; TR was forty-two, and FDR was fifty-one. I can think of no case of a leader, in the United States or elsewhere, experiencing Biden's scale of personal and political transformation at age seventy-eight.

My interviews suggest several mutually reinforcing explanations. The first was the historical situation that Biden inherited. As Elizabeth Warren told me, "FDR would not have been FDR without the Great Depression and Biden would not have been Biden without the pandemic." Sherrod Brown of Ohio, another progressive senator who has served with Biden since 2007, views him as a man of the center transformed by events. "The pandemic was the great revealer," Brown said, "He began to see that we needed big answers to big problems. You sit in that Oval Office with the statues and photos of earlier presidents, and you want to rise to meet the moment."

The Covid crisis and the deep recession that it created demanded large-scale direct public outlays. And Biden needed a drastic contrast with his predecessor. Trump was the ultimate faux-populist, an incompetent leader in a crisis as well as an aspiring autocrat. Trump talked about delivering for working people, but what he delivered was mainly racist nationalism. His policies were largely those of an orthodox corporate Republican. Both to succeed politically and to demonstrate his bona fides as working-class Joe, President Biden needed an expansive public investment program.

Yet Biden might have done what Obama did and promote modest anti-recessionary measures like the Recovery Act of 2010 that were "timely, targeted, and temporary," in the oft-repeated and self-defeating phrase of Obama's fiscal team. Obama's advisers, concerned about deficits, embraced large-scale public spending guiltily and reluctantly, as a last resort and at too meager a scale. But Biden went big.

A second key factor behind Biden's unexpected boldness was his determination to avoid repeating Obama's failure to seize his historical moment in 2008. I am reminded of the hip-hop musical *Hamilton* in two respects. Biden, unlike the Alexander Hamilton of the show, was far from young and scrappy. He had waited more than half a century. But he was not going to "miss my shot" to transform the economy the way Obama had missed his. And despite his personal closeness to Obama, Biden as VP had not always been "in the room where it happens." The elite team of Ivy League and Wall Street policymakers who worked for Obama did not treat Biden as part of their club. And when it came time for Obama to influence who he hoped would succeed him, he sided with his onetime bitter rival Hillary Clinton rather than his own vice president, explicitly discouraging Biden from running. All of that had to sting. Biden was determined to succeed in the areas where Obama failed. Now, the room where it happens is Biden's Oval Office.

A third reason for Biden's shift was the surprising influence of the progressive movement. The progressive critique of neo-liberal policies had been vindicated by events, and progressive groups had new energy and political credibility. The resistance to Trump that began with the massive women's marches and that bore political fruit in the midterm victories of 2018 was tactically brilliant at backing more moderate Democrats in moderate districts. But it was led by progressives.

Warren, Sanders, and their supporters played their hands astutely. Once they endorsed Biden, they traded loyalty to him for quiet influence. When Biden did win, he reciprocated. Warren was passed over both for running mate and for treasury secretary. Biden owed her. Several of Biden's policy ideas originated in proposals by Senator Warren. Several progressive appointees were Warren recommendations. Progressive leaders had far more impact than expected, both on policy and on personnel. Yet Biden was always careful to position himself as good old common-sense Joe. The practical problem is the disproportionate power wielded by a small number of centrists in a closely divided Congress. FDR had to contend with Southern racists who blunted his program. Biden has to deal with economic conservatives, the remnant of an era when Democrats disastrously allied with corporate elites.

Yet it would be a mistake to oversimplify the source of the blockage of congressional support for Biden's full program by a few center-right Democrats such as Joe Manchin. The deeper problem is that the Democrats' very narrow majority in both houses is result of long-term erosion of the Democratic Party as the credible champion of working people. When I worked as a Senate investigator in the 1970s, you could take a car trip from Washington State to Pennsylvania and hardly pass through a state with a Republican senator. Even better, all of the Democrats were progressives. More precisely, they were labor Democrats. Today, too many voters in those states vote Republican because they see little reason to vote for Democrats. In a classic chicken-and-egg problem, Biden could alter that calculus—if he can gain more traction with his New Deal program. As Manchin aptly put it, if you want to spend more money, "we have to elect more liberals."

Biden is still something of a centrist, by character, temperament, and long history. But in the years since 2016, the political center has moved left, with the utter discrediting of neoliberalism as a politics or a description of economic reality, plus the energy provided by practical progressives. On the eve of the 2020 election, the idea of a Green New Deal popularized by Alexandria Ocasio-Cortez was dismissed by many commentators as too radical and far-fetched. President Biden delighted progressives by embracing many of its elements. The Senate majority leader, Chuck Schumer, long disparaged as the senator from Wall Street, has been functioning as another born-again progressive and Biden's astute floor leader.

Biden's senior staff is another important factor in his shift to the left. Many of Biden's top advisers had mid-level positions in the Obama administration. Jared Bernstein, now an influential member of the Council of Economic Advisers, served as a junior member of the Obama economic team as the vice president's economist. Bernstein played the role of token progressive dissenter. He was regularly overruled by the imperious and far more centrist Larry Summers. Now, the progressive Bernstein is making policy; and he has several progressive allies in senior positions—put there by Biden. Elizabeth Warren's top economic adviser, Bharat Ramamurti, serves as deputy director of the National Economic Council in charge of consumer and regulatory affairs. Biden's regulatory appointees have been superb.

At the Federal Trade Commission, Biden appointee Lina Khan has begun to revive antitrust enforcement after a forty-year deep freeze, complemented by Jonathan Kanter as chief of the Justice Department's antitrust division. At the Securities and Exchange Commission, Gary Gensler is the most activist chair

in decades. At the White House, Tim Wu, one of our most astute critics of the multiple abuses of the big platform monopolies in telecom and the internet, is in charge of technology and
competition policy. These appointments are the most progressive
since FDR.

The shift in Biden's trade policy was personified by the appointment of Katherine Tai as U.S. Trade Representative. Tai
was not part of the crowd of good old boys from the Wall Street–
Washington revolving door who had carried out the trade orthodoxy under Clinton, Obama, and their Republican counterparts.
Fluent in Mandarin, she was the leading Democratic congressional staffer on trade. Earlier in her career, she worked at Office of
the United States Trade Representative on China negotiations.
Tai was a long-standing critic of free trade globalism as well as
the alliance between Wall Street and Beijing.

As an Asian American woman, Tai is also emblematic of a
fortuitous side effect of Biden's commitment to diversity in his
senior officials. In looking to appoint Blacks, Hispanics, Asian
Americans, and women, Biden has found himself fishing in
more progressive ponds. If you look hard, you might find centrists among people of color—but you are more likely to find progressives. For the most part, Biden appointed progressives to top
and second-level jobs. Just as racism had retarded progressivism
in earlier eras, Biden's quest to transcend racism got him a very
progressive cabinet and senior staff.

Other Biden policymakers who served under Obama have
moved left with the circumstances, like Biden himself. Brian
Deese, who heads Biden's National Economic Council, was a
mainstream centrist liberal when he served as chief of staff to
Vice President Al Gore and later to Vice President Biden. Deese
was best known as the person President Obama put in charge of
the national response to the Ebola outbreak in 2015. Like Biden,
Deese in office is a progressive.

The same is true of Biden's chief of staff, Ron Klain, who is close to Elizabeth Warren. Klain has been responsible for one progressive appointment and policy after another. Though there were plenty of center-right veterans of the Clinton and Obama years who were personally close to Biden, most of the key jobs went to relative progressives. Indeed, we dodged several bullets in who was not appointed to top staff and cabinet jobs. Among the Biden old boys are figures like Bruce Reed, who once headed the center-right Democratic Leadership Council. A counselor job was found for Reed at the White House, but it's not a serious power position. Steve Ricchetti, the epitome of a revolving-door lobbyist, is the one corporate Democrat in a senior White House post. He has done some damage to progressives by serving as a back door conduit for corporate lobbyists, but has also proven useful in legislative negotiations with Republicans.

A quiet source of influence was Biden's chief of staff from his Senate days, Ted Kaufman, who served out the last two years of Biden's Senate term in 2009–10 after Biden became vice president. Kaufman is by far the most progressive of Biden's personal inner circle. By no small coincidence, Biden put Kaufman in charge of personnel during the transition, and Kaufman took pains to make sure that most of the key posts went to progressives.

Biden's closest aides will tell you that he was always more progressive than you might think. During Biden's thirty-six years in the Senate, his rating from the liberal Americans for Democratic Action, based on a tally of key progressive votes, was equal to that of Ted Kennedy. "In Biden's mental model of how the economy works," one of his long-standing advisers told me, "there is a boss and a worker sitting at a table and the boss has far too much power, especially if the worker is not backed up by a union." In his support for the labor movement, Biden has said in so many words that workers need to join unions, a stance equaled only by FDR. The leader of a progressive think tank added, affectionately,

"Biden is so old that he pre-dates the neoliberal era. He came of age at a time when the working-class and union mentality was engrained in the Democratic Party."

One other factor in Biden's emergence as the most progressive president since Roosevelt is his personal story. At age twenty-nine, having just been elected to the Senate, Biden lost his wife and infant daughter when a tractor-trailer slammed into their car. On the eve of the 2016 election, he lost his beloved son Beau to cancer. Family tragedies can make a person hard-shelled, or compassionate. Americans who observed Biden in the campaign and in his first year as president sensed a man of genuine compassion who was deeply moved—and moved to action—by the suffering he saw during the pandemic year. Biden's personal modesty, and his determination to make his presidency about the American people and not about himself, was a welcome contrast to the bombastic narcissism of Trump. And it wore well.

Thus, against all odds, Joe Biden resolved to go big. And there is something breathtaking, after several decades of Democratic presidents distancing themselves from big government or progressive taxation or economic regulation, to witness a Democratic president resolving to reclaim a lost legacy.

For me, this story is also personal. I've been writing about the political and economic folly of Democrats moving to the corporate right for my entire career. If Democrats expect to be avant-garde on social and cultural issues, they have to deliver for the working class on economic ones.

I co-founded two institutions, the Economic Policy Institute in 1986 and the *American Prospect* in 1989, in an effort to restore some intellectual and strategic balance.

In 2008, I wrote my one bestselling book, titled *Obama's Challenge*. The book was a bit of a risk. I wrote it in the spring and summer, making the heroic assumption that the economy would collapse and that Obama would be elected. In the fall, the economy and the voters both obliged. The book was published in August and launched at the Democratic National Convention in Denver where Obama was nominated. My publisher and I joked that we'd either have a big hit or a big bonfire. In the book, I warned that Obama was at grave risk of being captured by the same center-right advisers who had led Bill Clinton to pursue policies that were perverse for working Americans. Obama evidently did not read my book.

But under the Biden presidency, I am enjoying the novel experience of actually having some influence, as opposed to being a voice in the wilderness vindicated by events. After Biden was nominated in March, I rather cheekily wrote a piece in the *American Prospect* titled "The Biden DNR List." DNR stood for "Do Not Reappoint," and the piece named twelve center-right former Obama and Clinton officials angling for high-level jobs, who under no circumstances should be reappointed by Biden should he win the presidency. Ten did not get appointed.

I then wrote a lengthy investigative feature about the top person on the list, Larry Summers, titled "Falling Upward." Summers dearly wanted to be in the new administration. He was hoping to be appointed Federal Reserve chair, the career-capper job that had twice eluded him. He was already part of the regular phone calls of Biden's nascent economic team, though the campaign had not listed him as an adviser. My piece pointed out that Summers's economic advice, time after time, had proved disastrous, from his pressure on post-Soviet Russia to rapidly marketize (producing depression, backlash, and Putin), to his leading the crusade for the financial deregulation that produced the 2008 collapse, to his embrace of perverse orthodoxy on budget balance and trade. Summers was also a terrible bully, as demonstrated in his disastrous and aborted tenure as president of Harvard. But he kept falling upward because he had powerful friends—just the sort of friends of whom a Democratic president should be wary.

The piece was widely circulated. Summers was quietly dropped from Biden's team. Several senior people called to thank me. After Biden took office, Summers repeatedly attacked Biden's spending plans as inflationary, doing the Republicans' bidding and usefully burning his last bridges to Biden.

I had written a similar piece in 2007, warning the next administration about the toxic influence of Robert Rubin. That piece was ignored, and several Rubin protégés and allies got top jobs in the Obama administration. Circumstances were not yet ripe for Democrats to jettison neoliberalism as an ideology and the conflicted Wall Street insiders who were its architects. It took Obama's own failures and their consequences for the wheel to turn—and Biden to redefine how to think about the economy and what Democrats stand for.

Stunningly, Biden jettisoned the entire set of neoliberal orthodoxies that had hobbled Democratic presidents since Jimmy Carter. Gone was the idea that deficits necessarily caused high interest rates and inflation. Gone was any illusion that we needed tax breaks for the rich in order to promote private investment. Public investment was needed at a large scale precisely because private investment had failed to serve the real economy and had enriched mainly manipulators, traders, and monopolists. Gone was the rhetoric that big government was not the solution, but the problem.

Biden also reversed the globalist fantasy that had been standard bipartisan policy since Carter. That view held that ever freer global commerce was a major source of greater efficiency and economic growth. This was nothing but the global counterpart of the domestic ideology of laissez-faire: markets work; governments don't. Beginning with Roosevelt, that was not the way the domestic economy actually operated. Government overrode market failures—and produced better outcomes—in multiple ways. Labor markets were regulated; unions influenced wages; government promoted economic development as well as basic science and R&D. There was substantial regulation to protect the environment.

Yet through some alchemy based on free trade theory, when markets were global they were said to be efficient after all. Domestic industry was sacrificed to globalized finance as outsourcing allowed end runs around labor regulation and undermined wages. Global financial deregulation supercharged domestic deregulation. Biden's predecessors were happy to let America's industrial economy implode for the sake of the ideal of free trade and the self-interest of multinational corporations and banks. It fell to Biden and his economic team to revise the globalist ideology in favor of coherent policies to rebuild American leadership in industry, technology, and supply chains, sacrificing free trade norms when necessary. Biden's version of Make America Great Again is for real, and without the racialized jingoism.

The American political system is now weirdly proceeding down two parallel and largely disconnected tracks. On one track, a competent national government is addressing a series of accumulated problems, with ingenuity and dedication. On the other track, one of our two national parties is not just working to block the administration's program, a posture that is unfortunate but not unprecedented; it is working to annihilate democracy.

Anti-democratic sentiments have poisoned not just cynical Republican politicians. They are evidently held by more than a third of the American people. The German ironist Bertolt Brecht captured the problem in a famous poem. In 1953, Brecht, a communist but a free spirit with little patience for bureaucracy, was living in East Berlin. Some functionary had expressed disappointment that the people were displaying insufficient enthusiasm for the party program. Brecht wrote a bitterly ironic poem,

"Die Lösung" (The Solution), in which he suggested that perhaps the government should dissolve the people and elect a new one.

But the irony is on Brecht—and on us. In World War II, the democracies defeated the fascist powers militarily. It is much harder when fascism lives in the hearts of your own people. Though a majority of Americans do not embrace the violent overthrow of democracy, at this writing a majority tell pollsters they will vote Republican for Congress, even as Republicans in office have become a quasi-fascist party that condones political violence. In November, the House Republicans defended the actions of a far-right member, Rep. Paul Gosar, who circulated a video depicting himself killing another House member, Alexandria Ocasio-Cortez. Just two Republicans joined Democrats in voting to censure Gosar, and Republican leaders swore retribution if they take back the House.

In August 2020, a seventeen-year-old self-appointed vigilante, Kyle Rittenhouse, brought an AR-15 assault rifle to Kenosha, Wisconsin, to "protect" local citizens from demonstrators protesting the police killing of a black man, Jacob Blake. He came in response to a call from a local far-right militia. Rittenhouse ended up killing two people and wounding another. In November 2021, after a jury accepted the self-defense alibi and acquitted Rittenhouse of all charges, several leading Republicans cheered the verdict and called Rittenhouse a hero. Three House members offered him an internship.

Most Americans do not feel safer in a society of vigilante justice. Most are appalled by the idea of a seventeen-year-old nominating himself to keep the peace with an assault weapon. The very idea is antithetical to the rule of law. But this is the society Republicans are promoting, with their stand-your-ground and open-carry laws. Yet in 2021, with Trump out of office, too many voters and media commentators treated partisan politics as a normal competition between two normal parties.

Recovery of democratic sentiments and norms will be a slow and protracted process that can begin only if Republicans are kept far from power and are made to pay the political price for their extremism. There is no plausible scenario in which traditional center-right Republicans take back their party. Despite several high-minded efforts by former Republican officeholders to deplore Trump and Trumpism, even going so far as to urge moderate Republicans to vote Democratic for Congress, all but an isolated handful of active Republican politicians are more thoroughly Trumpified than ever. Recovery of a decent America must be the work of Democrats.

In my review of FDR's legacy and that of the Democratic presidents who came after him, I draw several conclusions. There is immense latent public support for the use of activist government to better the situation of ordinary people. Foreign policy adventures, such as Vietnam, Iraq, and Afghanistan, can serve as distractions from domestic issues that play to Democratic strength, and can wreck the unity of the coalition needed to pursue domestic progressivism. So, obviously, can racism and the continuing legacy of slavery and segregation. But the big challenge is political economy.

In a democracy that is also a capitalist economy, there is an immense undertow of the influence of big money that undercuts possible policies. In the 1930s and '40s, there was a famous argument between John Maynard Keynes and his protégé, the more left-wing economist Michał Kalecki. As a matter of technical economics, Kalecki agreed with Keynes that it was indeed possible to have full employment in a capitalist economy. But as politics, he observed, the capitalists would never let you do it. When I was coming of age during the postwar boom, it looked like Keynes had the better of the argument. Today, Kalecki seems pretty persuasive. The Roosevelt era was exceptional, and it will take exceptional politics and leadership to restore a Roosevelt co-alition of the middle and working class that is economic and also multiracial.

This influence of capital in our economy undercuts progressive social and economic policies generally. Second-best and third-best policies that make it profitable for the private sector ostensibly to serve public purposes are often so cumbersome that they discredit both the policy and the government. But because of the pervasive corporate influence on Congress, these are the policies with the votes to get enacted. Health care policy is a costly and complex mess because it has to be run through so many for-profit players. Affordable housing is subsidized mainly by a tax credit that benefits wealthy investors via a process that makes actual development of the housing a nightmare of private bureaucracy. Decades of free-market propaganda have branded government as hopelessly inefficient. But in so many areas of public policy, direct government programs such as public education, public Social Security, public Medicare, and public power are more cost-effective than a mélange of subsidies and tax credits to private entrepreneurs and the cumbersome and unaccountable private bureaucracies that result. (See chapter 2.)

Biden needs to go beyond what even FDR achieved in containing a corrupted capitalist system, because that system today is the wellspring of so much policy failure, and so much political and economic inequality, as well as the corruption of too many Democratic leaders, all of which kindles support for Trumpism. Biden has done well in the "tax, spend, and invest" part of the New Deal legacy. He has shaken off the straitjacket of fiscal orthodoxy and used borrowing as well as taxing. His appointments have been progressive, thanks in part to the new influence of Democratic progressives. But he has barely begun the task of drastically reforming financial capitalism.

Trump got elected by channeling unfocused anger. The four

previous decades of declining living standards were also a time of social upheaval, with African Americans, women, immigrants, and LGBTQ Americans upending dominant hierarchies. Trump galvanized a classic fascist coalition of cynical elites improbably joined to people suffering lost material security or status. For most, the deeper driver of anger is economic, a distress Republicans can't cure and shouldn't be allowed to blur. Democrats can reclaim the FDR coalition by challenging extreme concentrations of wealth and power that have denied a decent life to ordinary Americans. Biden can be the avenging instrument of that anger, as Roosevelt was, or he will be the target of it.

A disclaimer: I mean this book as an assessment of the loss and rediscovery of the Roosevelt tradition, not as a hagiographic celebration of Joe Biden personally. A merciful god would not have placed Biden in this fateful role at this fraught moment. For one thing, our leader at this perilous time should be forty-nine, not seventy-nine, and looking forward to two robust terms. It isn't just that he is almost eighty; it's that some voters associate his age with the inevitable setbacks of a presidency in a narrowly divided country, and that costs him support.

Like any president, Biden has made some blunders, including the bungled final exit from Afghanistan. Other presidents have survived early setbacks. But today's circumstances are less politically forgiving. Roosevelt, Johnson, Carter, and Obama began their presidencies with historic tailwinds. Joe Biden, by contrast, faces severe political headwinds. After half a century in the political wilderness, it is exhilarating to find Biden emulating Franklin Roosevelt. But it is sobering to appreciate all the ways that this moment could be undone—and that Biden needs to go even Roosevelt one better.

2

Roosevelt's Fragile Revolution

I am a child of the New Deal. My parents bought their first home with a government-insured mortgage. When my father was stricken with cancer, the VA paid for his excellent medical care. After he died, my mother was able to keep our house thanks to my dad's veteran's benefits and her widow's pension from Social Security.

My generation grew up thinking of the system wrought by the Roosevelt revolution as normal. That system included decent payroll jobs, many with good health and pension benefits, and prospects for lifelong career advancement. It included homes that could be purchased on one income, even for the blue-collar middle class; as well as free higher education at public universities and no student debt.

But this seemingly permanent social contract was not normal; it was exceptional. It required rare constraints on the economic and political power of capital; the empowering of labor; and an activist state that enjoyed broad public support. Above all, it was fragile, built on circumstances and luck as much as enduring structural change.

When FDR took office in March 1933, he faced a devastated and despairing country. His first challenge was to restore a measure of hope. There were calls for him to assume dictatorial powers. While Roosevelt was assembling his first cabinet in Washington, Hitler was assembling his in Berlin.

In his storied first hundred days, Roosevelt got Congress to enact seventy-six pieces of legislation. Among them were laws creating the Tennessee Valley Authority, work relief measures such as the Civilian Conservation Corps and the Public Works Administration, the Agricultural Adjustment Act creating price supports for farmers, the Glass-Steagall Act making over the nation's banking system, and a good deal more. These measures and Roosevelt's own persona signaled and embodied a new role for government.

The early emblematic episode that best captures Roosevelt's intuitive political genius was his first fireside chat, a medium of Roosevelt's invention. It was a tutorial on banking.

Thousands of banks had failed since 1929, and tens of millions of Americans had lost their savings. The banking catastrophe deepened the collapse of local farms and businesses, as the depression fed on itself. In his first week in office, FDR got emergency legislation empowering him to temporarily close all the banks, a move prettified as a bank "holiday." The idea was to sort out which banks were solvent enough to survive, then provide them with cash advances from the Federal Reserve. But to do that, Roosevelt needed the help of a panicky public.

In the winter of 1932–33, desperate people had pulled their money out of banks, pushing more banks into insolvency. The Glass-Steagall Act created deposit insurance, but the FDIC would take effect only on January 1, 1934. So Roosevelt turned to his powers of optimism and persuasion. In his first fireside chat, Sunday, March 12, assuming the role of teacher, he explained:

I want to tell you what has been done in the last few days, why it was done, and what the next steps are going to be. . . . I owe this in particular because of the fortitude and good temper with which everybody has accepted the inconvenience and hardships of the banking holiday.

This was a fine case of FDR infecting the people with his own good humor. The public reaction to the bank closures was far from good-tempered. Roosevelt continued:

> When you deposit money in a bank, the bank does not put the money into a safe deposit vault. It invests your money in many different forms of credit—bonds, commercial paper, mortgages and many other kinds of loans. . . . A comparatively small part of the money you put into the bank is kept in currency—an amount which in normal times is wholly sufficient to cover the cash needs of the average citizen. . . .
>
> What, then, happened during the last few days of February and the first few days of March? Because of undermined confidence on the part of the public, there was a general rush by a large portion of our population to turn bank deposits into currency or gold. A rush so great that the soundest banks could not get enough currency to meet the demand. The reason for this was that on the spur of the moment it was, of course, impossible to sell perfectly sound assets of a bank and convert them into cash except at panic prices far below their real value. . . .
>
> It is my belief that hoarding during the past week has become an exceedingly unfashionable pastime. It needs no prophet to tell you that when the people find that they can get their money—that they can get it when they want it for all legitimate purposes—the phantom of fear will soon be laid. . . . I can assure you that it is safer to keep your money in a reopened bank than under the mattress.
>
> You people must have faith; you must not be stampeded by rumors or guesses. Let us unite in banishing fear. We have provided the machinery to restore our financial system; it is up to you to support and make it work. It is your problem no less than it is mine. Together we cannot fail.

The fireside chat was inspired and charming. According to FDR, "hoarding"—withdrawing your own money from a bank—was not quite shameful; it was merely unhelpful and "unfashionable."

Then something miraculous happened. The next morning, a Monday, when the banks reopened, the people who had been lining up at teller windows to take their money out began lining up to put money back in. They deposited $300 million in a single day. Runs on banks ceased. Weak banks were merged into stronger ones. With commercial banks heavily regulated and conflicts of interests prohibited under Glass-Steagall, bank failures became vanishingly rare. In 1933, some four thousand banks failed. In 1934, sixty-one did, of which just nine were FDIC-insured.

This was FDR at his best, and most revolutionary. He had a genius for taking charge in a good-humored and resolute way, characterizing transformative policies as merely common sense, delivering practical help, and winning over public sentiment—while Republicans predicted disaster and isolated themselves politically.

In the standard Roosevelt narrative, FDR restores hope. And he then goes about restoring the economy, using powers of government to put people back to work, and devising new public entities to accomplish what the private sector had bungled. He increases the prestige of the public sector and public solutions. He uses public deficits to restore purchasing power. He virtually invents a national system of social insurance with the Social Security Act. He puts the government on the side of workers' right to organize, with the Wagner Act, and then regulates wages and hours directly with the 1938 Fair Labor Standards Act.

The modern system of housing finance in America is the fruit of three pieces of New Deal housing legislation, which invented the long-term, self-amortizing mortgage. He created one agency, the

Federal Housing Administration (FHA), to insure mortgages so that banks would resume lending; a second agency, Fannie Mae, to buy mortgages and replenish bank cash; and a third agency, the Home Owners' Loan Corporation, to help underwater homeowners refinance mortgages. By 1940, homeownership rates had returned to pre-Depression levels. In the meantime, the Reconstruction Finance Corporation helped recapitalize corporations, and even put public members on corporate boards.

All of this is true—and all of it needs to be qualified. As the historian Jefferson Cowie observes, the New Deal was a temporary great exception to American political economy, and a somewhat unstable one. It wasn't quite transformative enough. The New Deal was in some respects collectivist, but the ideal of individualism persisted. It expanded government, but still relied mostly on the private sector. The fissure of race ran through it.

Roosevelt wasn't much of a Keynesian. He campaigned in 1932 calling for budget balance. In office, he was willing to borrow, but his deficits typically were only 3 or 4 percent of GDP, peaking at 5.4 percent in 1934. In early 1937, after winning the greatest reelection victory in the history of the republic, FDR succumbed to the counsel of fiscal conservatives, cutting spending and moving the budget to balance in 1938. The impact of this fiscal folly was an economic contraction known as the Roosevelt Recession, which caused unemployment to spike again to 19 percent and cost Democrats dearly in the 1938 off-year election. Throughout the New Deal, the obsession with fiscal orthodoxy never quite went away. As late as 1940, the unemployment rate was still 14.6 percent.* It took the accidental ultra-Keynesianism

---

* The unemployment statistics of that era counted people on work relief as unemployed. A Labor Department revision calculated that if such workers are considered employed, the unemployment rate drops to 12.5 percent in 1938 and 9.5 percent in 1940—still far from full employment.

of World War II, when deficits were as high as 25 percent of GDP, to finally produce full employment.

In areas where FDR did strive to be more radical, he was constrained by the persistent influence of capital. Roosevelt was not shy about correctly placing the blame for the Great Depression where it belonged—on Wall Street. In his rhetorical flourishes he spoke of driving the money-changers from the temple and welcoming the hatred of the wealthy. FDR's policies sought to rid the economy of the speculation with borrowed money and the conflicts of interest that had produced the crash. He only partly succeeded.

Prior to 1933, investment bankers, stockbrokers, and commercial bankers were often part of the same firm. In the 1920s, the pyramid of stock prices was driven by a combination of investor euphoria, unregulated speculation with borrowed money, conflicts of interest, and outright fraud. As subsequent investigations revealed, the large money-center banks would raise money to finance the floating of risky securities. Their retail arms would then peddle them to investors, using the prestige of the banks as a seal of approval, often knowing that they were high-risk. Once the bank unloaded the securities, it had already made its money, and the risk was someone else's problem. If investors wanted to take even greater risks and play the stock market "on margin," the bank's brokerage arm would lend them the money to borrow to buy stocks. When stock prices fell and the magnificent system of leverage went into reverse, the investor would be wiped out. When the financial pyramid collapsed like a house of cards in 1929, it took the whole economy with it.

Stock pools were a notorious abuse of the era. Insiders would borrow money, pump up the price of a stock, market it to retail customers as a sure winner, and then cash in before it crashed. The abusers were not small, fly-by-night operators on the margins of Wall Street. They were the largest and most prestigious banks.

The organizers of stock pools included the House of Morgan and National City Bank of New York. Just as the stock market was collapsing in October 1929, one of the worst pool operators, Albert Wiggin, president of Chase National Bank, shorted his own bank's shares, and made $4 million on the transaction.

If some of this rings a more recent bell, it is because exactly the same kinds of abuses were repeated in the run-up to the 2008 collapse—traders betting against their own customers; extreme leverage (borrowing by bankers) hidden from regulators; insiders creating high-risk securities using borrowed money, disguising the risk, and cashing out before pawning them off on bank customers; and new scams facilitated by the internet. How could this have happened? In the three decades before the 2008 crash, the New Deal's imperfect regulatory machinery had been gutted. For more appalling detail, see chapters 6 and 7.

Prior to the New Deal, there was no policing of securities markets except by the stock exchanges. But these were private clubs controlled by their member firms, and had little incentive to punish misconduct. Conflicts of interest, except in cases of outright fraud, were not illegal. In the aftermath of the financial collapse, Roosevelt and his advisers resolved to get very serious about regulating Wall Street.

There were two major prongs of the New Deal effort. The first, the Glass-Steagall Act, separated commercial banking from investment banking. Commercial bank deposits would be federally insured but also subject to strict supervision and regulation, as well as reserve requirements that limited their own leverage. No longer could commercial banks pawn off high-risk securities on gullible customers. They were also now subject to regulation of the interest rates that they paid on deposits, so that banks would not be able to bid against each other for market share by paying higher rates than their balance sheets could support.

The separation of commercial banking from investment banking worked well. So did the intensified regulation of commercial banks. What did not work so well was Roosevelt's equally far-reaching plan to regulate stockbrokers and stock exchanges. A core conflict of interest was that stockbrokers served both as agents of customers and as financial insiders who could use privileged knowledge to trade for their own accounts. Glass-Steagall broke the link with commercial banks but did not address the corruption within the stock brokerage industry.

FDR fashioned two other major bills to directly regulate broker-dealers and stock exchanges. But the 1933 Securities Act was weakened by industry lobbying. Its only real teeth were a series of requirements for disclosures. A company whose shares were publicly listed and traded had to make quarterly disclosures about its true financial condition, with officers and directors liable for material falsehoods or omissions. But this was far from sufficient. In 1934, Roosevelt went back to Congress for a second bill to complete the unfinished business of the first.

The Securities Exchange Act of 1934 proposed to separate brokers from dealers, rather as Glass-Steagall had separated commercial banking from investment banking, so that the same firms would not be both making markets in securities and selling them to retail customers. Floor traders were to be abolished. The Federal Trade Commission (FTC) was to be given broad authority over both stock exchanges and over-the-counter (off-exchange) stock and bond sales. The bill either strictly regulated or prohibited outright a variety of practices that had led to the crash, such as margin loans, insider trading, and stock pools. As Professor Joel Seligman, author of the definitive history of these proposed reforms, wrote, "If enacted, it would have ended all transactions on the exchange floor, transforming the Exchange into a clerical agency for execution for off-floor orders."

At the time, the public was far from sympathetic to Wall

Street. In a pseudo-populist tactic, the large New York firms used small regional stock exchanges and local banks to play on anti–Wall Street feelings, and enlisted local congressmen to make the case that the new legislation would harm smaller financial institutions. By the time the law was passed, industry lobbying had gotten rid of the provisions prohibiting insider trading; the system of broker-dealers and "floor specialists" was left intact; margin lending was permitted, subject to regulation by the Federal Reserve. And stock exchanges were allowed to regulate themselves. As a further protection against tough regulation, supervision of the financial industry was removed from the consumer-oriented FTC and lodged in a newly created agency, the Securities and Exchange Commission, which was expected to be more friendly to Wall Street.

Roosevelt, getting with the program, appointed to chair the new SEC a notorious pool operator, Joseph P. Kennedy. Some saw in this move a strategy of "set a thief to catch a thief." Others saw an olive branch to Wall Street and its allies in Congress. Either way, the new agency would be far from a tough regulator.

The failure to tightly limit a return to the abuses of the 1920s was compounded when the administration and Congress agreed to a seemingly innocent loophole in two pieces of legislation enacted in 1940 to regulate investment companies, what today would be called mutual funds. Under those twin laws, the Investment Company Act and the Investment Advisers Act, companies that sold stocks, bonds, and investment funds to the public were held to high standards of disclosure and capital adequacy. But the administration agreed to create a loophole for private investment companies, typically companies that served a wealthy family. These were exempt from all reporting requirements and could operate in secret.

Decades later, when the political balance of power and the ideological climate changed, the incomplete aspects of New

Deal financial reform allowed the repeat of the same kinds of abuses that crashed the economy in 1929. The small loophole in the Investment Company Act of 1940 was gradually widened to allow the creation of two entire predatory industries, hedge funds and private equity firms. Since private equity companies and hedge funds technically do not sell listed shares—they sell to so-called limited partners who are their de facto shareholders—they are exempt from either disclosure or safety and soundness regulation.

In a preview of the 2008 collapse, a hedge fund called Long-Term Capital Management nearly crashed the entire financial system in 1997. Unbeknownst to regulators, LTCM had borrowed so much money from different banks to finance its speculative bets that when one giant bet (that couldn't fail) went bad, its losses were on the verge of rendering every major bank insolvent. The Federal Reserve, exceeding its authority, called an emergency meeting of all the key bank CEOs and strong-armed them into creating a massive slush fund, to make LTCM and the larger banking system whole. The system held. Astonishing, no systemic reforms were pursued (see chapter 7). This was in the Clinton era, with its cheerleading for deregulation under Robert Rubin and Larry Summers. Today, even after the 2008 collapse and the Dodd-Frank Act of 2010, hedge funds and private equity companies are larger, more abusive, and more opaque than ever.

On paper, the New Deal legacy lives on. As the New Deal historian Eric Rauchway wrote, in a recent appreciation of FDR titled *Why the New Deal Matters*, "The New Deal matters because we all live in it; it gives structure to our lives in ways we do not ordinarily bother to count or catalog." As Rauchway declared, if you have ever earned minimum wage, relied on unemployment insurance, joined a labor union, used disability insurance, or put your money in an insured bank, "you have benefited from the New Deal."

Indeed, government at all levels spends close to a third of GDP, a statistic that has not fluctuated much since the 1940s. One of Roosevelt's greatest achievements, Social Security, keeps tens of millions of elderly Americans out of poverty. Workers in principle still have the right to unionize, under FDR's 1935 Wagner Act.

But FDR's legacy becomes more threadbare by the year. Unions have been decimated. The minimum wage is woefully inadequate. Conservatives have made it ever harder to qualify for disability assistance. Weak financial regulation makes it possible to lose your savings in countless other ways.

The labor organizer David Rolf of the SEIU likes to say, "Policy is frozen politics." Today's cold legacy policies are the result of yesterday's hot political struggles. But when the struggles themselves go cold, or the terrain of struggle is altered, the policy loses its vitality and becomes hollowed out. Capitalism, seemingly, is intensely regulated by a sea of agencies. Yet except for a few true public institutions with persistent staying power, such as Social Security, much of the New Deal legacy has been reduced to the form without the substance.

As conservatives never tire of pointing out, the tens of thousands of rules published in the Federal Register are more extensive than ever. But most regulatory agencies have been captured by the industries they regulate. So we have the worst of both worlds—the annoying red tape of regulation with few of the salutary public benefits.

The more complex the regulations, the easier they are to capture, since organized business and finance has legions of lawyers and lobbyists. The Glass-Steagall Act of 1933, which revolutionized the American banking system, ran 37 pages. The Dodd-Frank Act of 2010 consumed 848. This was not because the reformers of 2010 prized complexity, but because lobbyists for the bankers and their allies on Congress larded Dodd-Frank with waivers and exemptions to allow business as usual. A decade later, agencies were still finalizing rules and bankers were litigating them.

Even worse, publicly accountable regulators have ceded the public's business to privateers. Alongside public regulations have burgeoned unaccountable private bureaucracies that govern employers' rules for workers, corporate rules for investors, even contracts that consumers must sign agreeing to mandatory arbitration on terms favorable to the manufacturer if a product proves defective or dangerous. Regulatory agencies such as the Securities and Exchange Commission have delegated much of their enforcement to so-called "self-regulatory" organizations that are controlled by the regulated industry. If you complain about a fraudulent stockbroker, your complaint will be referred to something called FINRA, the Financial Industry Regulatory Authority, a private organization controlled of course by stockbrokers. Except in the most egregious cases, which are referred to the SEC, FINRA gives the broker a slap on the wrist. FINRA is a child of Roosevelt's failure to get a tougher Securities Exchange Act of 1934, which would have retained direct enforcement in the SEC.

Because of legislative and ideological compromises, public purposes in the realm of social policy are increasingly carried out by private, profit-making entities. This strategy of bribing industry to serve social goals creates gross inefficiency and complexity, which in turn makes government look bad. By contrast, Social Security is simplicity itself. Government takes in revenues, keeps track of benefits due, and cuts checks. The administrative costs are negligible. But the cut taken by the financial firms that manage 401k accounts can be a quarter to a third. The private insurers that carry out the Affordable Care Act add layers of cost and complexity, and maximize their own profits by finding deceptive ways to deny coverage and care. Because the ACA is a mixed public-private program, "government" then takes the fall as inefficient.

Housing programs use an array of tax credits and subsidies to developers that divert public money from actual housing, and make the process of building affordable housing blindingly complex for nonprofit developers. A loophole in the housing laws, demanded by the developers' lobby, allows a for-profit developer to take public subsidies and tax credits for twenty-five or thirty years to build and operate low-income housing—and then when the mortgage is paid off, the developer is free to either jack up the rents or sell the property to the highest bidder. Instead of creating permanent social housing, three decades of taxpayer subsidy creates only interim affordable housing and developer windfalls.

Even Medicare, one of the few *public* public programs, has been watered down and privatized in multiple respects, rendering it both less efficient and less equitable. The administration of Medicare claims is contracted out to private insurance companies known as Medicare intermediaries. "Medicare" drug benefits are insurance company products. The private insurance industry also won the right to use the trusted Medicare brand to offer for-profit health plans under a program of HMOs called Medicare Advantage, which now accounts for 43 percent of all Medicare subscribers. Nominally, these policies offer more coverage than standard Medicare. In practice, they profit by heavily "managing" (denying) care, targeting younger and healthier clients, and limiting allowable treatments, tests, doctors, and hospitals. And because the insurance industry has locked in these aspects of privatized Medicare, the process of moving toward something like true social Medicare for All is that much more difficult both politically and administratively.

By contrast, the early New Deal was deliberately public. Its public works programs were public. Its social housing was public. The Tennessee Valley Authority (TVA) and the great western dams were public entities—called "public power." Operation of the Civilian Conservation Corps (CCC) was not contracted out to a private vendor, like so many government programs today. It was a public agency.

Government reaped the prestige of these successes. The New Deal's ascendancy was built on a politically virtuous circle of policy achievements and public support, presided over by the magnificent man of the moment, FDR. New constituencies that Roosevelt helped mobilize, such as the labor movement and farmers helped by rural electrification and flood control, added to FDR's base of support.

Some of this chipping away of the New Deal system was the result of more than half a century of conservative efforts coupled with the resurgent political power of private business in both parties. Some of it was latent in fatal compromises that even Roosevelt had to make. Seen in structural terms, the New Deal was vulnerable to two potent undertows that would truncate its legacy and permit a restoration of the old order. One was the residual power of capitalists in a capitalist economy. The other was the stranglehold of white supremacy.

It is often forgotten that Roosevelt owed his nomination in 1932 to solid support from Southern delegates to the Democratic National Convention. In those years, it took two-thirds of delegate ballots to win nomination. This provision, retained at the insistence of the South, was intended to give Southern states a veto and assure that any nominee would support white supremacy. Before the rule was changed in 1936, it usually took multiple ballots and deals in smoke-filled rooms to produce a nominee. The great New Deal historian William Leuchtenburg writes, "At the 1932 Democratic Convention, where Roosevelt came within an eyelash of being denied the nomination because he did not appear to have enough momentum to reach the required two-thirds of ballots, he could thank steadfast southerners for pulling him through." Southern political bosses even backed FDR over one of their own, John Nance Garner of Texas, who became FDR's running mate.

Why Roosevelt? One reason was that the New York governor had made Georgia his second home. After being stricken with polio, FDR purchased and made over much of the town of Bullochville, which he renamed Warm Springs, where the pools gave him some respite from his paralysis. Politically, he made the most of his Georgia connection and used it to signal that he would be friendly to the white-supremacist South.

Some of the most vicious racists of the region were enthusiastic Roosevelt men. Congressman John Rankin of Mississippi went all out to deliver his state for FDR. Likewise South Carolina's James Byrnes, Huey Long of Louisiana (later FDR's bitter rival), and Memphis boss Ed Crump. The father of George Wallace helped raise money for Roosevelt. Richard Russell of Georgia, who would later warn Lyndon Johnson that support for civil rights would forever cost Democrats the South, termed FDR a "favorite son" as an honorary Georgian. Theodore Bilbo, one of the most vulgar of racists, was a strong Roosevelt supporter, telling an interviewer, "Any Mississippian not for Roosevelt and the New Deal ought to be ashamed of himself."

The Southerners who helped make Roosevelt president had every reason to believe that he would not use federal power to alter race relations in the South. And in Roosevelt's first term, he did not disappoint them. The wide array of relief agencies that delivered such practical benefits to the depressed rural South honored the tradition of segregation. Blacks were paid less than whites, and for the most part kept in separate work relief projects. The TVA employed not a single Black foreman or clerk, and Blacks were not permitted to live in the TVA's showcase community of Norris. Roosevelt refused the repeated entreaties of the NAACP to support anti-lynching legislation. When new programs were created, they were done so on a strictly segregated basis. One of the worst was FDR's otherwise admirable set of housing programs.

The New Deal represented the first time the federal government built public housing. It fell to Harold Ickes, a great racial liberal who was previously chairman of the Chicago NAACP, to negotiate the terms with the Southern Democratic legislators who controlled key congressional committees. The terms were very simple. Public housing complexes had to be rigidly segregated. In many cities of the North, working-class neighborhoods that were casually integrated were razed to make room for segregated housing complexes.

Richard Rothstein, author of *The Color of Law*, observes that it's a mistake to blame this policy entirely on the racism of the South. The Southern committee chairs, he points out, wanted to be sure that nothing in the New Deal would bring integration to the former Confederacy. But did they really care if New York or Chicago built integrated housing? The history of race riots and white antipathy to Black migrants in the North suggests that many Northern politicians wanted segregated public housing in the North as well.

New Deal racial policies for homeownership were even worse. In parts of the North well before the New Deal, mortgage lenders and homeowner associations had required racially restrictive covenants, obliging the owner never to sell to a Black person. But these were far from universal. When the New Deal created the Federal Housing Administration to insure and standardize mortgages, racially restrictive covenants and racial redlining maps became universal mandated practice. The policy, explicitly spelled out in the FHA 1935 underwriting manual, was not to insure mortgages that allowed Black homeowners into neighborhoods that were predominantly white. "If a neighborhood is to retain stability it is necessary that properties shall continue to be occupied by the same social and racial classes." This residential apartheid policy was reinforced by the secondary mortgage market created by Fannie Mae, and by the Home Owners' Loan Corporation, which refinanced mortgages with direct federal loans. The HOLC created color-coded maps to reinforce racial segregation.

These agencies were dead serious about enforcement. Rothstein recounts the case of a white San Francisco schoolteacher, Gerald Cohn, who purchased a home in Berkeley. For several months, before Cohn was ready to move in, he rented the house to a fellow teacher, Alfred Simmons, who was African American. The Berkeley police chief called in the FBI to investigate how a Black man had been able to infiltrate a white neighborhood. The FHA in turn falsely accused Cohn of deliberately purchasing the house with intent to rent to a Black family. This charge was rejected, but the FHA nonetheless blacklisted Cohn from receiving a future FHA mortgage. And this occurred in 1958, not in Birmingham but in liberal Berkeley. New Deal–mandated segregation cast a long shadow.

Thus the impact of the New Deal was to intensify and rigidify spatial segregation everywhere. That policy denied generations of African Americans the wealth-building opportunity of the great postwar housing boom, where government-mandated discrimination remained the law of the land until the 1968 Fair Housing Act. The landmark Supreme Court case *Shelley v. Kraemer* in 1948 held that racially restrictive covenants were not enforceable, but racial redlining, FHA exclusion, and the steering of Black homebuyers to Black neighborhoods persisted thanks to the legacy of New Deal policies.

Yet, to the outrage of the white-supremacist South, Roosevelt gradually became more of a racial liberal. To some extent this reflected the influence of Eleanor Roosevelt, who regularly spoke before Black groups and raised funds for the NAACP. And in fairness to FDR, his reluctance to take on white supremacy did not reflect his own views of race but his correct assessment of the sheer viciousness of racism in the white population, most especially in the white-supremacist South. That was evident in the ferocity of the reaction when Roosevelt in his second term began to make small and then increasingly bold gestures on behalf of oppressed Blacks.

In Atlanta, the Georgia legislature protested that regional officials of New Deal agencies were instructed to address Blacks as Mr., Mrs., or Miss. The Roosevelt Justice Department successfully petitioned the Supreme Court to invalidate the all-white primary, a Jim Crow device to keep Blacks from casting meaningful votes.

In 1936, FDR strongly backed the successful efforts to end once and for all the two-thirds rule in Democratic nominating conventions. Even more important were Roosevelt's increasingly overt efforts to weaken Southern racists by politically intervening to strengthen the South's white liberals. When the incumbent Senate majority leader, Joe Robinson, died, FDR strongly backed the liberal Alben Barkley over the segregationist Pat Harrison of Mississippi. Roosevelt even intervened in Southern primaries to elect and reelect relative liberals such as Claude Pepper of Florida and Lister Hill of Alabama to Senate seats.

The reaction of white Southern leaders was a sense of outrage and betrayal. The casually vicious language they used suggests the ferocity with which attitudes of white supremacy were held. As Senator Ellison "Cotton Ed" Smith recounted his experience at the integrated 1936 Democratic Convention, "I had no sooner taken my seat when a newspaperman came down the aisle and squatted by me and said, 'Senator, do you know a nigger is going to come out up yonder in a minute and offer the invocation?'

I told him, I said, 'Now don't be joking me, I'm upset enough the way it is.' But then, bless God, out on the platform walked a slew-footed, blue-gummed, kinky-headed Senegambian!" Smith walked out and didn't return.

In the 1938 South Carolina primary, Democratic Senate candidates outdid each other to demonstrate who was the more vigorous defender of white supremacy. Olin Johnston, challenging the notorious racist Smith, charged, "Ed Smith voted for a bill that would permit a big buck nigger to sit by your wife or sister on a railroad train." And Johnston was FDR's candidate in the campaign, as the lesser evil!

Georgia senator Eugene Talmadge began organizing Southern leaders to deny Roosevelt a third term. He convened an assembly of "Jeffersonian Democrats." On each delegate's seat was an article with a photo of the first lady, captioned: "picture of Mrs. Roosevelt going to some nigger meeting with two escorts, niggers, on each arm."

As war clouds gathered, relations between FDR and the white-supremacist South got even worse. Though it took a threatened march on Washington organized by the Black trade union leader A. Philip Randolph, in 1941 FDR issued an order creating a Fair Employment Practices Committee and banning racial discrimination in war production. When Roosevelt later countermanded an order by the comptroller general denying the FEPC operating funds, Talmadge called the move "a greater threat to victory than 50 fresh divisions enrolled under Hitler's swastika." Yet, in the election of 1944, when racist Southern leaders were livid at FDR's increasing racial liberalism, such was the gratitude of ordinary white voters for Roosevelt's leadership in ending the Great Depression that he carried every Southern state. Mississippi voted for FDR by a margin of seven to one.

I draw three conclusions from FDR's odyssey on race. The first is that leaders are capable of growing in office—Joe Biden being another prime example. The second is that we should never underestimate just how deeply rooted is racism in American society. The entire social and economic system in the South was based on white supremacy and the use of state-sponsored terror to enforce it. The slightest incursion, whether the integration of drinking fountains or the use of Mr. and Mrs. to address Blacks, could be the beginning of the end of the system. The massive resistance to ending white supremacy persists to this day.

But the third conclusion is more hopeful: when government delivers the goods for working people, that can sometimes be stronger even than racism. Most of the white Mississippians who voted overwhelmingly to reelect FDR did not like his increasing liberalism on race, but they voted for him anyway because of all he had done for them.

In some ways, World War II intensified the New Deal revolution. In other respects, the war short-circuited it. The wartime buildup finally produced the return to full employment that had eluded Roosevelt throughout the 1930s. It gave government even more emergency powers, such as temporary wage and price controls. The war created a system of national economic planning, in which civilian factories were requisitioned and refitted to produce ships, planes, tanks, and artillery, often financed by a much-enlarged Reconstruction Finance Corporation. The war raised marginal tax rates to 93 percent; it sidelined the private bond market, in favor of an agreement between the Treasury and the Federal Reserve in which the Fed would purchase whatever bonds the Treasury needed to sell, at a rate pegged at 2.5 percent. And the war further increased the role of trade unions as accepted social partners.

Unions had gained influence thanks to the Wagner Act and the militant organizing of the CIO. The war only reinforced their standing. The CIO leader and close FDR ally Sidney

Hillman was given several key jobs in the war mobilization. The government, in exchange for a no-strike pledge by union leaders, doubled down on enforcement of workers' right to unionize. If a corporation had war-production or supply contracts—and virtually all large corporations did—they were required to recognize their unions. For decades, labor organizers had on their walls an iconic photo of Sewell Avery, the president of Montgomery Ward, being carried out of his office for refusing to recognize the union. The wartime orders even helped integrationist industrial unions gain a foothold in the Deep South. Yet the wage controls and no-strike pledge also blunted union and worker militancy, and created conflicts between a leadership committed to Roosevelt and the war effort and a rank and file angry that they were not sharing in the immense profiteering by the military contractors who employed them.

Except for some gains for Black workers in war-production plants, progress on race was shelved for the duration. The armed forces remained strictly segregated. No Black officer could command a white enlisted man. A 1942 order required blood supplies for transfusions in military hospitals to be racially segregated. A token group of fifty Blacks was allowed into the Marine Corps in 1942, one of whom, a Marine named Edgar Huff, got a leave to visit his ailing mother in Atlanta. He was arrested in uniform by MPs when he got off the bus, for impersonating a Marine. They did not believe that a Black Marine could exist. Huff spent five days in jail before his commanding officer bailed him out.

Roosevelt, with the prodding of New Dealers in Congress and trade union leaders such as Walter Reuther, hoped that the wartime planning could be carried over into a postwar planned "reconversion" program for full employment. Economists were worried, and with good reason, that the return of 12 million GIs, coupled with the end of the extraordinary wartime economic stimulus, would cause the economy to sink back into depression.

The proposed Full Employment Act of 1945, sponsored by a great western progressive, Senator James Murray of Montana, called for a program of comprehensive national economic planning and a government employment guarantee, with direct federal employment if private sector job creation was insufficient. There were also elaborate plans for gradual, carefully paced decontrol of wages, prices, and rationing, to prevent an outbreak of postwar inflation.

All these grand plans and more were cut short by FDR's abrupt death in April 1945. Postwar economic planning was not to be. Wage and price controls were scrapped haphazardly. The Employment Act that eventually passed Congress in 1946 was mainly an aspirational document, with no concrete mechanisms to attain full employment.

Harry Truman, by instinct and political history, was less progressive than FDR. But when Truman's own election was on the line in 1948, he turned out to be a pretty good New Dealer, saved by the public's continuing affection for the Roosevelt revolution. Such was the power of the New Deal.

3

The New Deal's Long Half-Life

Like the New Deal itself, the twenty-five-year postwar period of broadly shared prosperity was a great exception to the history of capitalism. As Thomas Piketty's research has demonstrated, the norm in a capitalist economy is for wealth to become steadily more concentrated. But in the twenty-five years between 1948 and 1973, the economy not only grew at a rapid clip averaging more than 4 percent per year; it grew more equal. The bottom 20 percent increased their incomes at a faster rate than the top 20 percent. Despite the persistence of racial segregation and discrimination, even the gap between median Black and white incomes narrowed as well. That seems paradoxical. The reason the racial earnings gap narrowed is that the working class generally gained relative to the rich, and most African Americans were working class.

The great postwar boom was anchored by the changes wrought by the New Deal and World War II. With time, the reach of the long half-life of the New Deal would fade, as power shifted and institutions were altered. But that hollowing out would take more than a generation.

The most important shift was the revised status of labor and of capital. With the institutional power of the union movement guaranteed by the state, the regulation of the terms of employment by the Fair Labor Standards Act, and the return of full employment, a system of good payroll jobs with fringe benefits was now normal. Enactment of the anti-union Taft-Hartley Act in 1947 cost the labor movement some of its sharpest organizing tools to bring in new workers, but unions now represented one private sector worker in three, and that share would continue for another two decades.

On the other side of the power equation, capital was well regulated. For the moment anyway, bankers were serving the real economy and not feathering their own nests.

Finance was constrained in another sense. Relatively low interest rates coupled with the inflation of the early postwar boom, when consumer price increases averaged over 10 percent a year in 1946, 1947, and 1948, meant that owners of wealth were getting far lower real returns than usual. Real returns were often negative. The Great Crash had wiped out many large fortunes, and the recovery of the Dow to the levels of 1929 took until 1954. Inflation soon settled down to a range of 1–2 percent. The moderate inflation kept stock multiples in close alignment with the growth of the real economy. As a result of this "repression of finance," as the economists Carmen Reinhart and Kenneth Rogoff have termed it, the wealth of the wealthy during this era actually declined relative to the rest of the population.

Reinhart and Rogoff use that phrase disapprovingly; in fact it was a great achievement. The productive economy got all the investment capital that it needed, from low interest rates and retained corporate earnings. Meanwhile, the great wealth-accumulation engine for the non-rich—homeownership—burgeoned and housing values increased faster than inflation.

Some of the repression of finance was accidental—the result of the anomalous period of negative return on capital. But much of it was deliberate. Well-regulated financial institutions had (temporarily) lost their capacity to use corrupt schemes to pump up stock prices, so stock values rose more slowly than in eras of financial bubbles. Keynes had famously advocated, tongue slightly in cheek, "the euthanasia of the *rentier*," meaning that the economy should no longer be run in the interest of the investing class. That way, interest rates and capital costs for the productive economy could stay usefully low. During the postwar era, he got something of his wish.

Other aspects of the egalitarian postwar boom reflected a fortuitous rendezvous of deliberate policy with benign circumstances. Much of the postwar generation grew affluent thanks to good payroll jobs, cheap housing that appreciated faster than inflation, and free higher education. Today's young adults have none of these. That in turn has produced a hardening of class lines, as young people are more reliant on their parents for family head starts.

It's worth taking a closer look at the core elements of the greater economic equality that characterized the post-Roosevelt era.

Free higher education in America dates to the land grant colleges created in 1863 when Lincoln was president. These grew into our great state universities. Admittedly, it was easier to provide free public college when a much smaller share of the population went beyond high school. Yet in the postwar era, government policy explicitly helped, with measures such as the GI bill, which covered both tuition costs and living stipends so that returning veterans could attend college full-time. With more than half of young adults now going beyond high school, these policies will be more costly and harder to repeat politically—but not impossible. Several Western nations, with larger fractions of graduates than the U.S., still have free universities. Bernie Sanders's bill for free higher education would cost about $170 billion a year.

Good payroll jobs have been undermined by the weakening of trade unions, the use of globalism to outsource jobs, the rise of the gig economy, and the failure of government to enforce the terms of employment, owing to the increasingly common practice of employers disguising payroll jobs as independent contractor work, with far fewer worker rights. That could be altered by policy, but would take political shifts comparable to those of the Roosevelt revolution.

The great housing windfall will be hardest to replicate. The cheap housing of the postwar boom was one part deliberate policy and one part random events. The mortgage finance programs of the New Deal allowed working people to acquire homes. Also, the federally subsidized highway expansions and land clearance schemes of the postwar era allowed the conversion of cheap farmland into suburbia, producing more affordable homeownership. Then the inflation of the 1970s drove people to put even more money into housing, a real asset that was likely to hold its value. For two generations, homeowners enjoyed windfall gains as the worth of their homes kept appreciating faster than inflation. But the flipside of that gain is astronomical entry costs for their children and grandchildren, most of whom could not afford to buy the home they grew up in. Cheap farmland near cities is gone. Today's inflated housing prices mean that the great windfall of unearned housing wealth that so benefited my generation will never be repeated. So the use of homeownership as a way to help the non-rich accumulate net worth as well as an affordable place to live will require substantial public subsidy.

Among the several sources of the postwar boom, the temporary global supremacy of the U.S. economy was also a fortuitous event. The war had created the world's preeminent industrial machine. By 1945, all of America's economic rivals had been devastated. German and Japanese industry were set back for at least a generation. Victorious Britain, America's closest wartime ally, took longer to recover than defeated Germany.

There was no guarantee, however, that our military victory and towering industrial strength would lead to a postwar boom of shared prosperity. This outcome reflected good policy. American industry had also done well in World War I, while Europeans on both sides of the Great War suffered. But the postwar boom of the 1920s was lopsided and unsustainable, ending in the Great Crash. The fact that the twenty-five-year period of prosperity after World War II promoted security and opportunity for working people reflected the deliberate policies and power shifts of the New Deal system.

The Cold War played a paradoxical role. On the one hand, the Red Scare led to a purge of radicals from the labor movement, depriving the unions of some of their most militant and effective organizers. On the other hand, re-armament directed against the Soviets provided economic stimulus to spare the economy the predicted postwar recession. And it created a closet ministry of planning and industrial policy at the Defense Department. After the war's end, Congress rejected the kind of explicit economic planning proposed by the sponsors of the 1945 Full Employment Act. But the Pentagon operated as a convenient surrogate. The U.S. was now in an arms race with the USSR, and needed to be at the forefront of science and technology. The Defense Department functioned as an investment bank for new technology, as well as a guaranteed purchaser of output. Many of the weapons systems had commercial spillovers, producing U.S. dominance in everything from civilian aircraft to machine tools to semiconductors for more than a generation. Some economists referred to this as "military Keynesianism."

With the Cold War heating up and U.S. forces occupying much of Europe and Japan, the military never demobilized. Federal outlays in the first full year of peace, 1946, were 24.2 percent of GNP, more than in 1942. Postwar government spending never fell to the levels of the prewar New Deal. By the time federal spending briefly declined to a postwar low in 1948, of 11.2 percent of GNP, the great boom had kicked in. Returning

GIs and their families were buying homes and consumer durables. Unions negotiated for regular pay increases. Defying the fear of a postwar recession or depression, unemployment rates stayed below 4 percent, except for a brief spike to 6.6 percent in the mild recession of 1949.

When Harry Truman became president upon FDR's sudden death on April 12, 1945, the public saw a lesser man succeeding a greater one. Truman was no FDR. But Truman's gradual conversion into a full-throated New Dealer literally saved his presidency. His personal and political growth holds some lessons for understanding the parallel evolution of Joe Biden.

Truman came from Missouri, which had been a slave state. Jackson County, where he grew up, was as Southern in its racial outlook as any county in Mississippi. Truman's childhood was filled with tales from his mother and grandmother valorizing the Confederate cause, in which several of Truman's forebears had fought. One of his grandfathers had owned some two dozen slaves on a 5,000-acre plantation. Union troops had swept through his grandmother's home in 1863, threatening to kill his uncle Harrison, who was thirteen at the time. When young Harry, age twenty-one, came home in 1905 dressed in his new National Guard uniform, his grandmother reproached him, "Harry, this is the first time since 1863 that a blue uniform has been in this house. Don't bring it here again." Truman's mother once told an interviewer, "I thought it was a good thing that Lincoln was shot."

Truman casually used the N-word in his conversations and correspondence, as late as the 1940s. When the Daughters of the American Revolution refused to allow pianist Hazel Scott, wife of Harlem congressman Rev. Adam Clayton Powell, to perform at Constitution Hall in October 1945, in an echo of the famous Marian Anderson incident of 1939, Rep. Powell asked First Lady

Bess Truman to boycott a tea that the DAR had arranged in her honor. Mrs. Truman attended anyway, leading Powell to blast her as "the last lady of the land." Truman was furious at Powell and told an aide to "look up that damn nigger preacher and kick him around."

Truman had come to local prominence as part of the Pendergast political machine in Kansas City. Elected to the Senate in 1934 on the Roosevelt wave with the slogan "A New Deal for Missouri," he got along with both Northerners and Southerners, and is best described as a sometime New Dealer. He very narrowly won reelection in 1940. After a lackluster start, Truman distinguished himself as chairman of the Senate Special Committee to Investigate the National Defense Program, which he had proposed creating. It was soon known as the Truman Committee.

In 1941, as the defense buildup increased, Truman's committee held hearings around the country, investigating waste, fraud, and abuse on behalf of the taxpayer. It was the kind of non-ideological, quasi-populist effort against corruption that positioned Truman as champion of the little guy and brought him to prominence for the first time. The Truman Committee intensified its investigations once the U.S. entered World War II. It ended up saving taxpayers an estimated $15 billion. Though Truman's investigations occasionally embarrassed the Roosevelt administration, FDR found him a useful ally to put industry on notice and ward off scandals in military contracting. Even so, historians have never fully explained why an ailing FDR turned to Truman as his next vice president in 1944.

In that era, despite Roosevelt's personal popularity, other party leaders had substantial influence. Vice President Henry Wallace, a darling of the New Deal left but a quirky personality, had alienated key figures in Congress and the administration. By mid-1944, it was evident that Wallace would be dumped at the party's July nominating convention, with FDR's acquiescence. For a time, the segregationist Sen. Jimmy Byrnes of South Carolina seemed the front-runner to replace Wallace, but the party's liberal and labor leaders killed that idea. After a brief boom for the progressive Supreme Court justice William O. Douglas, Truman emerged as the compromise candidate, with FDR's quiet support. He had no working relationship with the president and was sworn in as VP less than three months before Roosevelt's death. FDR was in denial of his own precarious health. Truman was totally unprepared. He had not even been briefed on the atomic bomb.

For the party's progressive wing and for the common citizenry, Roosevelt's death was a crushing loss. Not only did Truman lack FDR's stature, he was far more centrist. In 1945 and 1946, Truman was preoccupied with foreign and military policy, and more hostile to Stalin and the Soviet Union than Roosevelt had been. On domestic affairs, Truman replaced several leading New Dealers with more orthodox figures and cut short the kind of planned and staged reconversion program that FDR wanted. He set back Britain's recovery by abruptly canceling the Lend-Lease program, reversing Roosevelt's assurances.

Truman faced the huge challenge of converting the war economy to peacetime, absorbing 12 million vets and millions more idled war-production workers without kindling either unemployment or inflation. Liberals criticized Truman for abandoning wartime wage and price controls too quickly. When unions pressed for deferred wage increases, Truman worried about the effect on inflation. In several high-profile conflicts, he seized factories and broke strikes in industries as diverse as coal, oil, steel, and railroads, invoking emergency wartime powers still on the books.

Liberals had hoped that the new Council of Economic Advisers created by the watered-down Employment Act of 1946 would be staffed by Keynesians. But Truman picked a far more centrist group, with Edwin Nourse of the moderate Brookings Institution as its first chair. So on a number of fronts, liberals felt that they had lost a champion in the White House. Conservatives didn't much like him either.

By the eve of the 1946 midterm elections, Truman's popularity rating was just 33 percent. He was widely viewed as a little man far out of his depth. A popular one-liner had it that "to err is Truman." Midterms are seldom great for the party in power, but 1946 was a blowout. Democrats lost fifty-four seats in the House and eleven in the Senate, allowing Republicans to take control of both chambers.

It was then that Truman began to rediscover the power of the New Deal. Far from accommodating himself to the Republicans, in the fashion of Clinton or Obama, Truman fought them at every turn. Despite his own bitter battles with labor just months earlier, he vetoed the anti-union Taft-Hartley Act, which was widely termed a "slave labor act." The act was passed over his veto, but he was more successful in blocking several other Republican bills. Truman emulated Roosevelt in championing public power. He nominated and fought hard to win Senate confirmation of the revered New Dealer David Lilienthal as head of the Atomic Energy Commission.

He emerged belatedly as a champion of civil rights, appointing a President's Committee on Civil Rights that delivered a landmark manifesto, "To Secure These Rights," and addressing the NAACP convention in June 1947, the first president to do so. There he delivered a tough speech promising the extension of basic rights "to all Americans." The Black press even compared Truman favorably to the beloved Roosevelt. "We cannot recall," editorialized the flagship *Pittsburgh Courier*, "when the gentleman who now sleeps at Hyde Park made such a forthright statement against racial discrimination."

The period of postcolonial awakening during the early Cold War influenced Truman's shift. It was an acute embarrassment to American diplomats that the U.S. was trying to persuade emerging third world nations—mostly nations of color—that the East-West conflict was a struggle between liberty and tyranny, while America's Black citizens were far from free. Civil rights groups made the most of this awkwardness by appealing directly to the United Nations. In a 1947 document written for the NAACP titled *An Appeal to the World*, at a time when the Truman doctrine was characterizing the world as half slave and half free, W.E.B. Du Bois wrote that "it is not Russia that threatens the United States so much as Mississippi; not Stalin and Molotov but Bilbo and Rankin." Against these contradictions and pressures from allies, Truman outraged the white South when he ordered the integration of the Armed Forces in July 1948.

With a landslide Republican win predicted for 1948, a campaign memo authored by top Truman advisers Clark Clifford and James Rowe in November 1947 urged Truman to double down on his New Deal liberalism. In June 1948, Truman used an invitation to accept an honorary degree at Berkeley to make a two-week whistle-stop rail tour of the American heartland. He began abandoning his rather stiffly delivered prepared texts and speaking off the cuff. He made a few impromptu gaffes, but audiences warmed to him. He covered 9,505 miles, delivering 73 speeches to an estimated 3 million people. A new persona emerged: Truman as plainspoken man of the people. His very ordinariness became a source of affection and strength.

At the party's Philadelphia convention in July, delegates from the newly created Americans for Democratic Action, led by Hubert Humphrey, pushed through a strong civil rights plank for the party platform. Truman had initially favored a much milder statement on civil rights explicitly designed not to alienate the white South, but he didn't actively oppose the stronger one. Humphrey deftly trapped Truman into going along, and then effusively praised him as a civil rights president.

With the Cold War percolating, Americans for Democratic Action had been founded as the voice of the noncommunist New Deal left, in contrast with the Wallace wing of the party that accepted the support of the far left. ADA for a time wanted to dump Truman, beseeching Dwight Eisenhower to run as a Democrat. But as Truman became more of a progressive, the ADA became his fervent supporter. Without the pressure of both the ADA and the Wallace forces further left, Truman would have been much more inclined to seek the safe center.

The passage of a strong civil rights plank was the final straw that led to a convention walkout of key Southerners, who formed their own States' Rights Party with Sen. Strom Thurmond of South Carolina as nominee. Their vicious and racist language of betrayal, recalling the white South's turning against Roosevelt, once again showed just how far the nation had to go to extirpate racism.

Meanwhile, the newly created Progressive Party, made up of people who rejected Truman's Cold War policies, nominated former vice president Wallace. With defections on both Truman's left and right, commentators were convinced that Truman was doomed. But then, at the Democratic Party convention, Truman announced the brilliant tactic of calling Congress back into session so that he could dramatize the stark differences between Republican policies and his own. With this surprise announcement, according to historian David McCullough, "the cheering and stomping in the hall was so great he had to shout to be heard."

Truman then sent Congress a Rooseveltian package of

legislation on housing, aid to education, a higher minimum wage, development and reclamation programs for the South and West, increased Social Security, and expanded public power, knowing that none of it stood much chance in the Republican Congress. Truman biographer Alonzo Hamby writes, "The objective was not to achieve compromise legislation that all sides would probably consider flawed. It was to underscore ideological differences for a presidential campaign. In achieving this goal, Truman was extraordinarily effective. The dozen or so significant vetoes he issued in 1947 and 1948 underscored differences between Democrats and Republicans on issues such as income equity, labor-management relations, regulation of business, and the New Deal welfare state."

The observation bears repeating. *Truman's strategy was not to achieve flawed compromise legislation but to underscore differences*—differences that would play to Democrats' latent strength as the party of the common people. Truman's strategy, in short, was 180 degrees from the one that Clinton and Obama pursued, and more like Biden's.

Truman's attacks on the "do-nothing 80th Congress" created the lasting image of "Give 'Em Hell" Harry, friend of the average American. Meanwhile, the timing of the Soviet Union's Berlin blockade and the coup in Czechoslovakia, both in 1948, undermined the credibility of Wallace's peace campaign, while Truman's strong support for civil and labor rights kept most Northern Black and trade union voters from defecting to Wallace. Several leading Southern moderates refused to join the Dixiecrats, while the Republican nominee, Gov. Thomas Dewey of New York, succumbed to front-runner disease and ran a safe, lackluster, and uninspiring campaign.

In September, Truman embarked on an extended version of his earlier two-week rail tour across America. This time, he would spend a total of thirty-three days and cover 21,928 miles.

With each stop, his attacks on the Republicans grew more scathing, and his subject was nearly always the economy and the Republicans' role as the party of obstruction and privilege. In Dexter, Iowa, he told a crowd of some ninety thousand people, "I wonder how many times you have to be hit on the head before you find out who's hitting you? . . . These Republican gluttons of privilege are cold men. They are cunning men. . . . They want a return of the Wall Street dictatorship. . . . I'm not asking you to vote for me. Vote for yourselves."

In Denver, he told a crowd of 25,000 people in front of the State Capitol, "Republicans in Washington have a habit of becoming curiously deaf to the voice of the people. They have a hard time hearing what the ordinary people of the country are saying. But they have no trouble at all hearing what Wall Street is saying."

Speaking in Congressman Sam Rayburn's hometown of Bonham, Texas, Truman said, "Our primary concern is for the little fellow. We think the big boys have always done very well, taking care of themselves. . . . It is the business of government to see that the little fellow gets a square deal. . . . Ask Sam Rayburn how many of the big-money boys helped when he was sweating blood to get electricity for the farmers and the people in the small towns."

This was a language of progressive populism, even of class warfare, another idea regularly disparaged by commentators. But this language accurately describes the relationship of Wall Street to Main Street in 1948 as in 1933—and in 2022. Progressive populism turned out to be winning politics for Truman, not because it was cheap demagoguery but because there were real differences between the parties, and major public issues at stake whose resolution one way or the other would benefit different classes of voters. Billionaire Warren Buffett once quipped that there is indeed class warfare in America, "but it's my class, the rich class, that's making war, and we're winning." It is astonishing how the commentators who cluck about the perils of mentioning class routinely ignore endemic class warfare from the top, and even more astonishing that recent Democratic presidents before Biden blurred which side they were on.

Before the 1948 election, *Newsweek* polled fifty leading political journalists to see who they thought would win the presidency. All fifty predicted Dewey. A tiny handful of journalists traveling with Truman sensed the change in public opinion. "There is an agreeable warmheartedness and simplicity about Truman that is genuine," Richard Strout wrote in his *New Republic* column. Three months earlier, on the eve of the Democratic Convention, the same magazine had run a cover piece on other possible Democratic nominees to save the party from certain defeat, headlined "Truman Should Quit."

Conventional wisdom would say that with a Democratic president's public-approval ratings in the 30s and the Republican Party controlling Congress, the obvious strategy would have been for Truman to move toward the Republican ideology and program. This was the view that paralyzed Democrats for decades. By contrast, Biden has connected not just with his inner Roosevelt, but with his inner Truman.

On Election Day, Truman won a respectable 303 electoral votes compared to Dewey's 189. He won the popular vote by more than 3 million. The States' Rights Party carried just four Southern states—Alabama, Louisiana, Mississippi, and South Carolina. Truman won the rest of the Old Confederacy, including Georgia, North Carolina, Virginia, and Texas. Despite Truman's increasing liberalism on race, white voters in most of the Deep South (where almost no Blacks could vote) were motivated mainly by the practical help the New Deal had delivered to that depressed region, and stayed loyal to the Democrats. Truman thus split hard-core racists from voters who could be moved by economic issues. Biden's success will depend on whether he can repeat that trick.

On the left, the Wallace Progressives carried no states, but did win more than half a million votes in New York, which cost Truman the Empire State. Truman, in sum, managed to hold together most of the Roosevelt coalition by running as a New Dealer. With neither of the protest parties running candidates down-ballot, Democrats took back an astounding seventy-five Republican seats in the House and nine in the Senate, recapturing both chambers. Voters who defected to Thurmond or Wallace still voted heavily Democratic for Congress.

It's worth a second look at the Cold War and the international economic policy of the Truman era, and their impact on subsequent political events. At the Bretton Woods conference of 1944, the objective was to fashion a global economic and financial order consistent with the policies and principles of New Deal progressivism at home. That meant, above all, dethroning private finance as a source of both speculation and deflation, in favor of public capital and a system biased in favor of full employment and steady economic growth. The Bretton Woods design included fixed exchange rates, so that there would be no speculative pressure on nations to pursue perverse austerity policies that would drag down each other's economies.

Bretton Woods also envisioned a global currency, a World Bank as a source of public capital, and an International Monetary Fund (IMF) to lend money to spare debtor nations perverse austerity policies. These latter three measures were not fully carried out. A global currency was impractical—the U.S. dollar ended up serving that role; the Marshall Plan proved a larger source of reconstruction capital than the World Bank; and the IMF soon began attaching onerous conditions to its loans. Nonetheless, Bretton Woods created a system of managed globalism—the opposite of the laissez-faire approach to trade and global finance that prevailed in the calamitous 1920s and returned in the neoliberal era that began in the 1980s. This Bretton Woods system undergirded Europe's miraculous postwar recovery with public capital and managed markets, in marked contrast to the postwar economic crises after World War I—and after 1989. It was the slow undoing of that system that led to global neoliberalism.

Ordinarily, the Treasury Department is the home of the most conservative officials of an administration. Democratic presidents, seeking to reassure financial markets, typically place Wall Street veterans at the Treasury. This was the practice of Johnson, Carter, Clinton, and Obama. But the Roosevelt Treasury was the home of radicals. The most radical was Harry Dexter White, the top U.S. government architect of the postwar global financial system. White was a close collaborator of the chairman of the Bretton Woods conference, John Maynard Keynes. In the 1930s, White had been either a communist or a fellow traveler. When that history surfaced, he was forced to resign as the designated head of the new IMF. The Truman administration had little enthusiasm for the third of the proposed Bretton Woods institutions, an International Trade Organization that would subordinate free trade to high labor and social standards. The ITO treaty was never presented to the Senate for ratification, and the organization was stillborn.

As treasury secretary, Truman appointed conservative Fred Vinson of Kentucky to succeed FDR intimate Henry Morgenthau, a progressive who had been a strong backer of White and Bretton Woods. Will Clayton, a onetime cotton broker and trader who had served in a variety of wartime posts, displaced White as the key Truman official on international economic policy. Treasury ceased being the home of economic radicalism; it reverted to its usual role as the home of economic orthodoxy. But the inertial power of the Bretton Woods system, the power of the dollar, and the logic of government-to-government assistance for European recovery prevented an early reversion to global laissez-faire. That would come later, with Democrats Clinton and Obama as cheerleaders. Biden has also begun reversing that.

Roosevelt had hoped, naively to his critics, that the close wartime alliance with the USSR as well as with Britain would continue. He placed great faith in the new United Nations, whose inauguration he never saw, having died two weeks before the UN's first meeting in San Francisco. Roosevelt believed that the Soviet Union had legitimate security interests, and that if these could be met Stalin would pose no threat to the West.

At the eight-day Yalta meeting with Churchill and Stalin in February 1945, with Roosevelt's health failing, he went a long way toward meeting what he considered Stalin's valid needs. He agreed to partition of defeated Germany into occupation zones, giving Stalin a foothold in what would soon harden into the satellite German Democratic Republic (DDR). He agreed that there had to be a government friendly to Russia in postwar Poland, though there were also supposed to be free elections. Roosevelt also made the Soviet Union eligible for postwar reconstruction aid. But Stalin soon acted to deny not just Poland but all of central and Eastern Europe freely elected governments in favor of puppet regimes. To Republicans, Yalta became symbol and substance of why Democrats could not be trusted on national security.

Just two weeks in office, Truman faced his first foreign policy crisis. Stalin, in open defiance of the Yalta commitments, formally recognized the provisional, pro-Soviet Polish government in Lublin, installed courtesy of the Red Army, and made clear that there would be no elections or even token inclusion of representatives of the free Polish government in exile in London, as agreed to at Yalta. Truman requested a meeting with the Soviet foreign minister, V.M. Molotov, who agreed to stop over in

Washington en route to the UN San Francisco conference. After having been briefed in detail by FDR's top Russia advisers, the plainspoken Truman dressed down Molotov in the most undiplomatic language. At the end of the meeting, according to the transcripts, Molotov said, "I have never been talked to like that in my life." To which Truman responded curtly, "Carry out your agreements and you won't get talked to like that."

While it enhanced Truman's stature, the Cold War and the emergence of the once-isolationist U.S. as leader of the Western alliance would later result in overreach and misadventures that split the Democratic coalition. It would give Republicans, who could not win on pocketbook issues, a cudgel to intimidate Democrats.

On both domestic economics and international politics, one can speculate endlessly about what might have happened had FDR lived to complete his fourth term. The postwar reconversion might well have been more systematic, with a measure of national planning. Given FDR's prestige, the huge Republican gains in the 1946 midterm elections might have been smaller. That in turn could have prevented such policy reverses as the 1947 Taft-Hartley Act, which weakened the labor movement by allowing states to opt out of full union shops through "right to work" measures, allowed management to propagandize workers in union elections, and prohibited boycotts of target companies by other friendly unions. After Taft-Hartley, organizing in the South ground to a halt.

With regard to the Soviet Union, even before Roosevelt's death the assumptions of Yalta were rapidly being overtaken by events, notably Stalin's expansionist moves against western and central Europe. Even FDR's softer-line officials, such as Henry Stimson, George Marshall, and Dean Acheson, were moving toward a tougher posture. America's use of nuclear weapons against

Japan in August shocked Stalin, who immediately saw them as creating a strategic imbalance against the USSR, and led him to redouble his own preparations for East-West conflict. Because of FDR's close wartime relationship with Stalin, some of the worst Cold War polarization might have been averted had FDR lived, but there is no doubt that containment of an expansionist USSR would have been the prime foreign policy challenge. Entire libraries have been written on this subject and I do not propose to settle the question here.

For our purposes, it's worth noting three Cold War legacies that have disadvantaged Democrats and progressivism ever since Roosevelt's death. First, the welfare state became a warfare state. Military spending tended to crowd out new domestic outlays. This was especially pronounced as the Vietnam escalation undercut LBJ's Great Society.

Second, the Cold War promoted secrecy, enhanced unchecked executive power, gave freer rein to the likes of J. Edgar Hoover and domestic spying, and made America less of a robust democracy. The blowback from the Cold War included the secret subsidy of CIA front groups such as the National Student Association and FBI efforts to weaken the civil rights movement. It led to tens of billions of dollars in secret outlays for agencies not subject to the usual congressional or public scrutiny, and to U.S.-orchestrated coups in several countries. There is a direct line from the creation of the CIA in 1947, to the use of the illegal domestic counter-intelligence operation known as COINTELPRO to disrupt the civil rights movement and the New Left in the 1950s and 1960s, to the faked Gulf of Tonkin attack, to the secret courts created in the 1990s and expanded in the aftermath of the attacks of September 11, 2001.

Third, the Cold War put Democrats on the defensive generally. It shifted the terrain of political argument from domestic economic issues, where Democrats played to strength, to the communist threat where Republicans could gain ground by charging that Democrats were too soft. "Who lost China?" was a big theme in the 1950 and 1952 campaigns. Richard Nixon, as a rising young congressman, ridiculed "Dean Acheson's College of Cowardly Communist Containment." Nixon would never have gotten much traction as a domestic anti–New Dealer. Roosevelt's programs were simply too popular.

Eisenhower, as a president somewhat above party, was savvy enough not to mess with any of the Roosevelt legacy. Ike had a Democratic Congress for six of his eight years as president. He worked with Democrats to expand Social Security. Banks stayed regulated; taxes stayed progressive; and Ike did not go after trade unions. But where the Cold War was concerned, Ike appointed people like the Dulles brothers, who were ultra-hardliners on foreign policy. This, in turn, made Democrats more defensively hawkish. Eisenhower also made no progress on civil rights, leaving that massive challenge to the future Democratic administrations.

In 1960, John Kennedy actually ran to Nixon's right on anticommunism (no small feat), railing against an invented "missile gap" that had supposedly developed on the Republican watch. Historians later found that there was indeed a missile gap—in the United States' favor. Kennedy also brought the world to the brink of nuclear war in the Cuban Missile Crisis. As Kennedy began to pursue détente with the Soviets during the last year of his life, there is evidence that he was contemplating a U.S. exit from Vietnam. The more he learned about Vietnam in late 1963, when he played a very hands-on role, the more Kennedy appreciated that all the official reports about how well the war was going were fabrications.

We can never know for certain. But we do know that Lyndon Johnson, a master of domestic policy, had none of Kennedy's self-assurance on foreign affairs. Where Kennedy had been increasingly skeptical of the hawks who in 1963 were already calling for a massive infusion of U.S. ground troops, Johnson placed his faith in them.

The Democratic defensive unease on national security policy combined with the unfinished business of racial justice to destroy Johnson's presidency. The Vietnam debacle also shattered the New Deal coalition and the hopes of progressive Democrats for half a century.

4

LBJ's Tragedy and Ours

Lyndon Johnson revived the New Deal coalition and its philosophy of activist government, working to complete FDR's unfinished business on economic and racial justice. After the Kennedy assassination, Johnson won election in 1964 by an even greater popular majority than Roosevelt had achieved in 1936. In LBJ's refashioned coalition, newly enfranchised African Americans displaced white racists, establishing the Democrats as a consistently progressive party on race as well as economics. He was easily primed to be the greatest president since Roosevelt.

And then, Johnson's Vietnam debacle smashed it all to pieces—a demolition whose ideological and political reverberations undermined progressivism for more than half a century. Joe Biden, against long odds, has begun to put the coalition and its policies back together.

At the peak of his political and moral authority, Johnson addressed a joint session of Congress in March 1965, imploring the legislators to pass a Voting Rights Act. He recalled his time as a young schoolteacher in Cotulla, Texas, where most of his pupils were migrant Mexicans. "My students were poor and they often came to class without breakfast, hungry. They knew even in their youth the pain of prejudice. They never seemed to know why people disliked them. But they knew it was so, because I saw it in their eyes." He added:

I never thought then, in 1928, that I would be standing here to-night, in 1965. It never occurred to me in my fondest dreams that I might have the chance to help the sons and daughters of these students and people like them all over the country. But now I do have that chance—and I'll let you in on a secret—I mean to use it.

The speech, combined with Johnson's trademark arm-twisting and the heroic efforts of civil rights activists shaming Southern sheriffs, led Congress to finally enact the Voting Rights Act. The address came just days after the epic Selma to Montgomery march, in which police blocked, hosed, and killed demonstra-tors. The marchers, led by Martin Luther King Jr., made it only on the third try, and only after Johnson's attorney general, Nich-olas Katzenbach, had warned Governor George Wallace that the marchers would be accompanied by federal marshals if necessary.

Johnson's speech included these startling words:

What happened in Selma is part of a far larger movement which reaches into every section and State of America. It is the effort of American Negroes to secure for themselves the full blessings of American life.

Their cause must be our cause too. Because it is not just Ne-groes, but really it is all of us, who must overcome the crippling legacy of bigotry and injustice.

And we shall overcome.

Here was the president of the United States embracing the anthem of a radical movement, valorizing people who were breaking the law to secure the Constitution. In the November 1964 election, Johnson had carried all but six states—the four that went for Strom Thurmond in 1948 plus Georgia and Barry Goldwater's home state of Arizona. Goldwater voted against both civil rights acts. The racist migration to the Republican Party had already begun.

LBJ's popular landslide win produced FDR-scale majorities of 295 to 140 in the House and 68 to 32 in the Senate. Now, in addition to the civil rights agenda, Johnson could set about completing the New Deal. In the years between 1964 and 1968, landmark Great Society legislation included the Economic Opportunity Act, education aid measures, Medicare and Medicaid, and federal support for education and mass transit, as well as several consumer and environmental measures and three landmark civil rights acts.

Like the New Deal before it, the Great Society, even without the diversion of Vietnam, was incomplete, and not without flaws that would later prove more serious. In the war on poverty, there was fierce division between those who wanted the heart of the strategy to be full employment and those who pursued what critics termed a "deficiency model" of improving the skills and habits of the poor. (In the ultra full employment of World War II, the poor learned on the job, and became middle class.) This argument would reverberate for the next half-century, with Congress passing inadequate training programs while labor markets and wages went to hell. Medicare was a great achievement, but it was also flawed from the outset because even LBJ could not get Congress to pass true national health insurance. As I suggested in chapter 2, Medicare only became more watered down and less efficient with time.

Yet given the constraints of the time, the Great Society was heroic. Johnson went far beyond his predecessors in appointing African Americans to senior government posts, capped by his appointment in 1967 of the first Black justice to the Supreme Court—and not a safe Black as some of his advisers had urged, but the longtime leader of the NAACP Legal Defense Fund, Thurgood Marshall. He had crossed a personal Rubicon. As he resolved to champion civil rights, Johnson warned his white-supremacist mentor, Sen. Richard Russell of Georgia, "I'm going to roll over you. You've got to get out of my way. I'm not going to cavil or compromise."

"You may do that," Russell prophetically replied. "But it's going to cost you the South."

Russell did not get out of Johnson's way. Though LBJ tried to cajole Southern Democrats to support the 1964 Civil Rights bill, no senator from the Old Confederacy voted for it, except the great Texas progressive, Ralph Yarborough. Even Southern senators who were progressive on other issues, such as Albert Gore Sr. and J. William Fulbright, voted against it. Such was the persistent power of white supremacy.

This was the same Lyndon Johnson who opened his 1948 Senate campaign with a speech in Austin, declaring: "The so-called civil rights program is a farce and a sham—an effort to set up a police state in the guise of liberty. I am opposed to that program. I voted against the so-called poll tax repeal bill . . . against the so-called anti-lynching bill . . . against the FEPC." He added he was an enthusiastic supporter of the Taft-Hartley Act.

How to explain Johnson's odyssey? His early roots were New Deal. In 1935, he became the youngest state director of FDR's new National Youth Administration. When Johnson won a House seat at age twenty-nine, in 1936, he won it as a New Dealer. But in his political rise he was shamelessly opportunist. In his 1948 campaign, when polls showed that only 14 percent of Texans supported Truman's civil rights program, Johnson pandered to racists. In his early years as a U.S. senator, Johnson shamelessly pandered to racists. He became majority leader after just seven years in the Senate, as a protégé of the notorious white supremacist Russell. Johnson's reputation was that of a skilled wheeler-dealer with no core convictions. He was also a close friend of the oil and gas industry, which had bankrolled his rise.

When the Kennedys invited Johnson to run for vice president in 1960, a shrewd if cynical move that helped JFK clinch the nomination on the first ballot and narrowly carry Texas in the razor-thin general election, nobody thought of Johnson as a racial liberal—or as liberal at all. For the New Deal wing of the party, which was supporting Hubert Humphrey, Kennedy wasn't much of a progressive and Johnson was worse.

But in November 1963, Johnson's opportunism took a radically different form—the conviction that his place in history was to complete the work of the New Deal and of Reconstruction. If Truman's shifts sometimes suggested whiplash, Johnson's was the most stunning turnabout in American political history. Biden's odyssey is tame by comparison.

Johnson's shift on race had actually begun while he was vice president. Kennedy, temporizing on civil rights, had put LBJ in charge of the toothless President's Committee on Equal Employment Opportunity. But Johnson decided to make some waves. Speaking in Gettysburg, on the hundredth anniversary of Lincoln's Gettysburg Address on Memorial Day 1963, Johnson said, "The Negro today asks justice. We do not answer him—we do not answer those who lie beneath this soil—when we answer 'Patience.'" The speech was front-page news in the *Washington Post*. The Kennedys, who were counseling patience, were not amused. They had brought in Johnson to conciliate the white South, not to upstage his cautious president.

In the early morning hours of November 23, Johnson told his aide Jack Valenti, "I'm going to pass the Civil Rights Act. . . . I'm going to fix it so that everyone can vote, so everyone can get all the education they need. I'm going to pass Harry Truman's health care bill."

In death, the martyred Kennedy proved more effective to the cause than in life. In his first speech to Congress on November 27, Johnson declared, "No oration or eulogy could more eloquently honor President Kennedy than the earliest possible passage of the civil rights bill for which he fought for so long. We have talked long enough about equal rights in this country. It is now time to write the next chapter and write it in the books of law."

The evening of Kennedy's funeral, November 25, Johnson phoned Martin Luther King, not as a courtesy call but to talk strategy. "I'll have to have you-all's help," Johnson told King, according to the recorded transcript. "I never needed it more than I do now." It was the beginning of what Johnson understood as a necessary alliance between the power of the presidency and the power of radicals on the ground. Johnson continued his tactical and moral alliance with King, in defiance of J. Edgar Hoover's insistence that King was a communist and the FBI's repeated efforts to blackmail King.

Kennedy had been a deep disappointment to civil rights leaders. In a shrewd tactical campaign move in late October 1960, Kennedy had phoned Coretta Scott King to express sympathy and support, when her husband was in jail and Mrs. King feared for his life. Kennedy had promised in the 1960 campaign to end housing discrimination "with the stroke of a pen," but waited more than two years to issue an order prohibiting federally insured housing loans from considering race. As civil rights agitation intensified, polls showed that half of Americans felt the country was moving too fast on race, and Kennedy had other priorities. Not until 1963 did Kennedy send Congress the draft of the first major civil rights act, which seemed hopelessly stalled. Kennedy was having trouble getting legislators to pass far more routine legislation.

Yet the 88th Congress that passed the Civil Rights Act of

1964 was the very same Congress that President Kennedy had been unable to move. Under Johnson's leadership, seventy-one senators voted cloture to end a record seventy-five-day filibuster and force consideration of a civil rights measure for the first time since the filibuster had been invented. Johnson managed to enlist the Republican Senate leader Everett Dirksen, with a medley of patronage benefits, to bring along twenty-nine Republican votes for passage, more than half of the Republicans then in the Senate.

The Civil Rights Act of 1964 prohibited racial discrimination in employment and in restaurants, hotels, and other forms of public accommodation. It outlawed discrimination in all forms of transportation. Opponents of the bill added gender discrimination, in the hopes of sinking the measure. But the strong support of women actually helped the bill to pass. Left out of the bill was federal enforcement of voting rights, a deal-breaker for several of the senators whose votes Johnson needed for cloture. Johnson would have to come back to get voting rights when he had a more heavily Democratic 89th Congress, and after the conscience of the nation was pricked by the scenes of police violence on the great march from Selma to Montgomery.

The day after Johnson's voting rights speech on March 15, 1965, several Southern senators met for breakfast. "Did you hear ol' Lyndon say, 'We shall overcome'?" asked an incredulous Spessard Holland of Florida. The relative moderate Lister Hill of Alabama turned to Richard Russell: "Dick, tell me something. You trained that boy. What happened to that boy?" "I just don't know, Lister," Russell said ruefully. "He's a turncoat if ever there was one."

Lyndon Johnson and Martin Luther King Jr. remained the closest of allies—until King broke with Johnson on Vietnam in August 1965, just months after the triumph of the Voting Rights

Act. Their relationship never healed, and the breach only widened. It was one more cost of the war.

The Voting Rights Act of 1965 gave the Justice Department extensive authority to overrule Southern strategies for denying Blacks the vote. All changes in voting systems in states or jurisdictions with racist histories required Justice Department pre-clearance to be sure that they did not have an overt or covert racial purpose. Opponents of the bill compared it to the gross regional affront of Reconstruction. And they were right. Reconstruction, before it was aborted, required the occupying Union Army to protect the new Black right to vote and hold office. After a century of Jim Crow tactics to deny Blacks the franchise, the Voting Rights Act provided for an occupation of Justice Department examiners, countermanding state sovereignty. They set up registration offices in post offices, government buildings, and where necessary in trailers. They hired local Blacks as registrars. "It was a segregationist's worst nightmare," wrote Ari Berman in his authoritative history, *Give Us the Ballot*, "Blacks registering other Blacks in the Deep South."

In Mississippi, the percentage of eligible Blacks registered went from 6.7 percent in 1965 to 59.7 percent in 1967. And in 1968, Congress passed the third of the great civil rights bills, the Fair Housing Act, prohibiting discrimination in the sale or rental of housing. But like the original Reconstruction of 1865–77, what scholars began to call the Second Reconstruction would prove to be short-lived. Such was the power of white supremacy—and yet another cost of Vietnam destroying the reconstituted progressive governing coalition.

For all his political cunning, Johnson was a deeply insecure man. That insecurity, paradoxically, would drive him relentlessly both to redeem Roosevelt and Lincoln—*and* to deny him the nerve to avert the Vietnam debacle. As his biographer, the astute Doris

Kearns Goodwin, quoted Johnson reflecting on his first days in office, "I took the oath. I became President. But for millions of Americans I was still illegitimate . . . a pretender to the throne, an illegal usurper. And then there was Texas, my home, the home of both the murder and the murder of the murderer. And then there were the bigots and the dividers, and the Eastern intellectuals, who were waiting to knock me down before I could even begin to stand up."

He would show the doubters, by doing it all—winning civil rights, and winning Vietnam. He was mindful of the Republican charges that the Democrats had fought a futile war in Korea, and "lost China," and tolerated communists in government. Johnson was willing to face down Richard Russell, but he was intimidated by the foreign policy advisers he inherited from Kennedy. He kept them in office even as he replaced most of the domestic policy team: Secretary of State Dean Rusk, a longtime Cold War hawk dating to his days as assistant secretary of state during Korea; Defense Secretary Robert McNamara and National Security Adviser McGeorge Bundy, neither with experience conducting an actual war; and the most hawkish of them all, Bundy's assistant W.W. Rostow, whose advice for saturation bombing of North Vietnam in 1962 and for an invasion of the North in 1963 had been roundly rejected by Kennedy.

In LBJ, Rostow found his man. Johnson promoted Rostow to replace Bundy in 1966.

David Halberstam tells this story in his definitive history, *The Best and the Brightest*:

> After attending his first Cabinet meeting Johnson went back to his mentor Sam Rayburn and told him with great enthusiasm how extraordinary they were, each brighter than the next, and that the smartest of them all was "that fellow with the Stacomb on his hair from the Ford Motor Company, McNamara." "Well,

Lyndon," Mister Sam answered, "you may be right and they may be every bit as intelligent as you say, but I'd feel a whole lot better about them if just one of them had run for sheriff once."

When Johnson became president, Vietnam was a second-order foreign policy problem far less urgent than U.S.-Soviet relations. The French, Indochina's colonial power, had suffered a humiliating military rout at Dien Bien Phu in 1954 and had pulled out. Vietnam was partitioned into two states, pending a final settlement. Ho Chi Minh's government in the North, influenced at least as much by nationalism as by communism, was determined to unify the entire country. The Saigon government was corrupt and unpopular, and the Viet Minh was controlling ever more of the countryside.

In November 1963, the U.S. had just 16,752 "advisers" in Vietnam, up from 300 when JFK took office. It was becoming increasingly clear that the U.S. would have to either become more directly involved, or cut its losses as the French did, accept that Ho Chi Minh would eventually control the entire country, and try to contain the geopolitical repercussions. Kennedy's advisers had been divided, and the person in the room most skeptical of deepening U.S. military involvement was often Kennedy.

On Johnson's third day in office, he received a visit from the new U.S. ambassador to Saigon, Henry Cabot Lodge, who warned him that things were "going to hell in a hand basket," as Johnson later summarized the meeting. Two days later Johnson signed a National Security Action Memorandum reaffirming the U.S. commitment in Vietnam against the "externally directed and supported communist conspiracy," one of the many lies the U.S. government told itself about Vietnam. As Johnson recounted the meeting with Lodge to his aide Bill Moyers, he told Lodge "to go back and tell those generals in Saigon that

Lyndon Johnson intends to stand by our word. . . . I want 'em to get off their butts and get out in those jungles and whip hell out of some Communists. And then I want them to leave me alone, because I got some bigger things to do right here at home."

Tragically, this remained Johnson's view until the end. Vietnam was a distraction that could be solved only by winning, despite the mounting evidence that it could not be won. Johnson kept receiving reports from senior officials warning that the war could not be won. He chose to listen to those who insisted that it could.*

It is ironic in the extreme to view the Vietnam debate of the mid-1960s from the perspective of the geopolitical realities of 2022. When South Vietnam did fall to Ho Chi Minh's forces in 1974—this after an elaborate Nixon-Kissinger dance of "Vietnamization," after the humiliating defeat of the world's greatest military power by lightly armed guerrillas, and after the loss of more than fifty thousand American lives and millions of Vietnamese lives—not much else happened geopolitically. There was a bloodbath in Cambodia, but it was more the spillover from the Vietnam War than a falling domino.

At the time, China was viewed as Ho Chi Minh's sponsor and puppeteer; the loss of Vietnam would be a victory for China. Today, China is the world's other leading superpower, but for

---

* "The South Vietnamese are losing the war to the Viet Cong. . . . No one has demonstrated that a white ground force of whatever size can win a guerrilla war—which is at the same time a civil war between Asians—in jungle terrain in the midst of a population that refuses cooperation to the white forces (and the South Vietnamese) and thus provides a great intelligence advantage to the other side." Undersecretary of State George W. Ball to Lyndon Johnson, memorandum, July 1, 1965.

reasons that have nothing to do with Vietnam. Indeed, China's ascension, as a communist dictatorship that has mastered the arts of predatory state capitalism, has thrived on a policy blunder by American neoliberal presidents that ranks right up there with the Vietnam War. President Clinton in 2000 agreed to admit China to the World Trade Organization as a normal trading nation, with no serious concessions by China either on human rights and democracy or on China's illegal subsidies of export products. In the case of U.S. Cold War policy toward the USSR, capitalism and national security worked in tandem. The Soviet Union was both a geopolitical threat and there was no money to be made trading with the Russians. In the case of China, the rising threat was evident. But there is plenty of money to be made underwriting investment partnerships and offshoring production to low-wage Chinese workers. So capitalism trumped national security. Biden is the first Democratic president to reverse that indulgence.

Vietnam today is a friendly trading partner of the United States, and a major supplier and customer of American industry. It continues to be ruled by the Vietnamese Communist Party, and is no geopolitical threat to anyone. The Hanoi government's main foreign policy concern, ironically, is to avoid domination by China.

A personal memory from the Johnson era: In 1965, I was a graduating senior at Oberlin. The Gulf of Tonkin Resolution, based on a faked incident providing the rationale for a major escalation, had passed Congress overwhelmingly in August 1964. American troops in Vietnam were now up to 184,000, and the U.S. was losing both the war and public support for it. Our commencement speaker was Martin Luther King Jr., who was to receive an honorary degree. Another honorary degree recipient was Dean Rusk. This presented student leaders with a dilemma. We could boycott commencement and dishonor Dr. King, or perhaps let the event proceed and find a way of expressing our displeasure at Rusk and at the college administration for honoring him.

At length a compromise was negotiated. We would let the commencement proceed with no protest, in exchange for a lengthy off-the-record discussion on Vietnam between several student leaders and Rusk. We twenty-two-year-olds pitched Rusk a plan. Suppose the United States ended the war by recognizing Hanoi as the government of all Vietnam, in exchange for a guarantee by the great powers of unified Vietnam's neutrality? Rusk scoffed at our naivete. The histories later revealed that Roger Hilsman, the dovish assistant secretary of state for Asia, had proposed much the same deal, and had been excoriated by Rusk for "taking the communist line."

A decade and millions of lives later, the United States ended the war on far less favorable terms. Six decades later, Vietnam is a docile communist nation and a leading U.S. trading partner. It was an early reminder that outsiders sometimes know better than insiders; that insiders often live in an echo chamber of self-reinforcement of their own myths. This proved to be true on other foreign policy questions, such as Iraq and Afghanistan. It was no less true on economic policy, where the profession's best and brightest led Democratic presidents from one neoliberal folly to another, oblivious to the political fallout as well as the mistaken economics. It would have been a lot better if one of the economists had run for sheriff once.

The collateral damage of Johnson's decision to wade deeper into the quagmire of Vietnam is staggering. First, of course, it destroyed his presidency. Johnson went from a series of domestic policy triumphs in 1966 and 1967 to abdicating in 1968. Protests against Vietnam became the all-consuming passion of an idealistic generation. Young people who had worked for civil rights and social justice in the early part of the decade became consumed with Vietnam. The idealism fragmented into several irreconcilable pieces.

In 1963 and 1964, my generation could hope that civil rights would be redeemed; that an engaged government could address a range of social problems from education to medical care to poverty. After grieving the loss of a young president who was becoming more attractive and liberal, we saw in Johnson a leader in personal passage, who paradoxically could succeed where Kennedy had failed. But by 1968, the *annus horribilis* of the King and Kennedy assassinations, the cities burning, the Dump Johnson movement, the police riot of the Chicago convention, another round of barbaric bombings and escalations, and finally the election of Richard Nixon, it had all turned to shit.

The civil rights movement split into integrationists and Black nationalists. The student movement fragmented into nihilists, Yippies, summer-of-love narcissists, peaceful protesters versus purveyors of violence, and several factions of radical and liberal antiwar activists who didn't trust one other. Some of the labor movement was against the war. Other unionists, steeped in patriotism, saw the protesters as traitors. Hard hats versus hippies became an indelible image of the era.

In October, Hubert Humphrey was at last gaining ground in the polls, but he had waited a little too long to break with Johnson and he was unable to paper over the divisions. A lot of disgusted liberal Democrats stayed home. The white backlash against civil rights gained force against divided national Democrats. Third-party racist candidate George Wallace, building on the Strom Thurmond vote of 1948, carried five Southern states and forty-six electoral votes. Wallace also did shockingly well in the industrial Midwest, winning huge votes in the very same counties where Donald Trump would defeat Hillary Clinton. Among the Northern states where the Wallace vote was larger than the margin by which Nixon beat Humphrey were California, Connecticut, Florida, Illinois, Indiana, Missouri, New Jersey, Ohio, and Wisconsin.

Had there not been the Vietnam fiasco and the bitter divisions it spawned, Johnson would have been able to complete more of his economic program; there would not have been guns crowding out butter; he (or Humphrey) would have had a unified party; and Wallace would not have pulled so many Northern votes. There would have been a white-supremacist protest vote, but mostly confined to the Deep South as in 1948.

In short, but for Vietnam it is hard to imagine Richard Nixon being elected president. Even before his election, Nixon had taken a leaf from the George Wallace playbook, with what was euphemistically known as his Southern Strategy. Unlike Wallace's raw racism, Nixon's was dog-whistle racism—a rhetoric of law and order and of states' rights. By the election of 1972, when Wallace was not on the ballot, Nixon's strategy had worked perfectly. He carried forty-nine states, including all of the Deep South. Republicans have pursued the same strategy ever since.

The campaign of George McGovern, and the lessons drawn from it, amounted to still more collateral damage from the Vietnam disaster. McGovern was no flaming radical. He was a mainstream New Deal/Great Society Democrat, as well as a patriot. He had served as Kennedy's director of the Food for Peace program. He had been a bomber pilot in World War II. But as Nixon continued to prosecute the war, with more atrocities in Southeast Asia and more mayhem at home, McGovern emerged as the champion of the antiwar movement, and managed to win nomination overcoming a rigged convention process.

McGovern had committed the sin of encouraging young protesters to work "within the system," thus shaking up the party establishment. The young McGovern delegates, finding a paucity of Blacks and women in the regular Chicago delegation and still smarting from the police violence of 1968, seated a rival delegation led by Jesse Jackson over the official Daley machine. Many party regulars sat out the 1972 election or even supported Nixon. This included much of the labor movement, now a somewhat more conservative movement as the conservative AFL had absorbed the radical CIO, and federation president George Meany had pretty much stopped new organizing in favor of what was called business unionism.

When Nixon, who had resorted to the electoral dirty tricks that later cost him his presidency, trounced McGovern, it was taken as an object lesson that the Democrats should never again nominate a radical. In fact, leaving aside the Vietnam schism, McGovern's views were closer to those of Harry Truman than Bernie Sanders. But memories of the 1972 blowout made "McGovernite" a term of scorn and would disadvantage progressive candidates for 1976 and beyond.

In principle, the 1965 Voting Rights Act still protected the Black franchise. But Republican presidents beginning with Nixon did their best to undermine it. For a single generation, political scientists could conclude that where the First Reconstruction had been destroyed, the Second Reconstruction was sticking. In several Southern states, a coalition of newly enfranchised Blacks and white moderates committed to economic development and better public education was able to elect moderate liberal governors and senators.

Democrats were able to win the presidency with two racially liberal Democratic governors emblematic of the New South—Jimmy Carter and Bill Clinton. North Carolina elected several progressive governors. Even Mississippi elected a moderate Democratic governor, Ray Mabus, with Black and white support. Seemingly, the biracial South sought by Lincoln was at last becoming reality. A retrospective 2009 book by two political scientists was titled *The Triumph of Voting Rights in the South*.

But all this was gone by the time that book went to press. The vaunted Second Reconstruction lasted barely a generation. Rather like a neighborhood that is briefly integrated before it flips from all-white to all-Black, the Deep South went from one-party domination by racist Dixiecrats, through a brief period of biracial governing coalitions, and then back to one-party domination by white-supremacist Republicans.

When Ronald Reagan ran for president in 1980 against Jimmy Carter, the dog whistle became a megaphone. He chose Neshoba County, Mississippi, where three civil rights workers had been murdered in Freedom Summer 1964, to open his campaign, declaring, "I believe in states' rights." The message was hard to miss. Reagan carried the entire South, except for Carter's home state of Georgia.

By the time Donald Trump was elected in 2016, every state in the Deep South had a trifecta of Republican governors and majority-Republican legislature in both houses. These states resorted to extreme gerrymandering and voter suppression to keep things that way. Everywhere in the thirteen states of the Old Confederacy, at least two-thirds of whites typically voted Republican.

Nominally, the Voting Rights Act of 1965 was regularly renewed. Originally set to expire in 1970, it was extended several times, most recently in 2006 when it was re-authorized for twenty-five years. Yet behind the apparent progress were relentless maneuvers by white Southern officials looking to dilute Black voting rights. The number of voting changes submitted by states for Justice Department pre-clearance increased from 110 in 1970 to 1,357 in 1972. Under Democratic presidents, the Justice Department tended to be vigilant. Under Republican presidents, it increasingly sided with the racist South.

White Southern officials used a range of devices to hold down Black voting, such as moving polling places, manipulating legislative districts, and toughening ID requirements. They shifted from district elections to at-large elections to dilute Black voting strength. Mississippi required voters to re-register for each election and changed the state's primary law to require a runoff, so that a Black candidate could not win with less than 50 percent of the vote.

For a time, civil rights advocates found redress in the courts. That changed as Nixon, then Reagan and both presidents Bush named conservative judges. The notorious strategy of using at-large voting districts to dilute local Black voting strength was common throughout the South. In 1978, the U.S. Commission on Civil Rights surveyed a sample of seventy-five localities with Black majorities and at-large systems, but no Black elected officials.

Under Carter, the Justice Department resisted these ploys and the courts tended to side with civil rights litigants. But in the landmark 1980 case of *Mobile v. Bolden*, in which lower courts had held that Mobile's system of at-large voting was patently discriminatory, the High Court held that plaintiffs had to prove not just discriminatory effect but discriminatory intent. The Fifteenth Amendment, Justice Potter Stewart wrote for the majority, "does not entail the right to have Negro candidates elected, but prohibits only purposefully discriminatory denial." The intent of the city fathers was all too obvious, as Thurgood Marshall pointed out in dissent, but as long as they could disguise it, the voting system was constitutional. The 6–3 majority included four new Nixon justices: Burger, Powell, Rehnquist, and Blackmun.

It did not take long for Southern racist officials to act on the court's invitation. The ploys became more audacious, and the Reagan administration either turned a blind eye or actively colluded to promote voter suppression.

The coup de grâce came with the *Shelby County v. Holder* ruling of 2013. The county filed suit after the Obama Justice Department had rejected a transparent ploy in which officials redistricted the town council in Calera so that the town's lone Black council member would lose his seat. Shelby County officials appealed. In a 5–4 decision written by Chief Justice John Roberts, the Supreme Court concluded that the South had changed and that pre-clearance was a dire and no longer necessary intrusion on federalism. The decision was not even a day old before Southern states and localities resurrected racist voting schemes that been overruled by the Justice Department, making a liar out of Roberts.

As a clerk to his predecessor, Chief Justice William Rehnquist, Roberts surely knew that he was attributing racial progress to the effects of the Act itself. Ruth Bader Ginsburg wrote in dissent, "Throwing out pre-clearance when it has worked and is continuing to work is like throwing away your umbrella in a rainstorm because you're not getting wet."

With the Voting Rights Act crippled, Texas legislators revived a scheme that had been rejected as discriminatory by the Justice Department, defining permissible (and racially targeted) forms of voter ID. Gun licenses were accepted, but not college ID cards. In Alabama, public housing ID was dropped from the list of acceptable forms of ID.

North Carolina's legislature eliminated student IDs and public employee ID cards. It shortened periods for early voting, expanded purges of the rolls, narrowed provisional voting, and eliminated pre-registration drives for high school students. In 2014, Thom Tillis, the Speaker of the North Carolina House and architect of the voter suppression bill, narrowly defeated Democrat Kay Hagan for a U.S. Senate seat. His 48,000-vote win was far less than the number of citizens who had been prevented from voting by the state's new restrictions.

The 2016 presidential election was the first to be held without the protection of the Voting Rights Act. Most states controlled by Republicans, twenty-four in all, had introduced new voting restrictions. Of these, thirteen states added more restrictive voter ID requirements, eleven made it more difficult for citizens to register, seven cut back early voting. In Florida 182,000 voters were purged; in Indiana, 481,000; and in Ohio, over 2 million. The purged voters were disproportionately poor, Black, and Hispanic.

In two of the most closely fought states in 2018, the Democrat would very likely have won races for governor in Georgia and governor and senator in Florida but for voter purges. Between 2012 and 2016, Georgia removed some 1.5 million voters from the rolls. Georgia also selectively closed or shortened hours of polling places in predominantly Black areas. In the aftermath of Biden's narrow victory in 2020, several Republican-led states doubled down on voter suppression and added strategies to explicitly politicize the election count.

Had the gutting of the Voting Rights Act and all the suppression that followed not occurred, we can imagine a very different history. More Blacks would have been able to vote at all levels and have their votes translate into political representation and the exercise of power. More Southern states, counties, and cities could have had positive experiences with New South governing coalitions. Hard-core racists would have been politically isolated. The Second Reconstruction might well have stuck. Without the Nixon presidency, there would have been four fewer conservative justices on the Supreme Court undermining voting rights and a great deal more. Now, the Biden administration and the progressive movement need to undertake a Third Reconstruction, but in far less benign judicial and legislative circumstances.

In terms of the cycles of American history, the power of the Roosevelt revolution and what it achieved for ordinary Americans was sufficient to entrench progressive Democratic presidents for twenty years; and with the exception of two years under Eisenhower, to keep Democratic control of Congress all the way until 1980—a total of forty-eight years. But for the Vietnam fiasco, progressive Democrats as the normal party of government would likely have continued into the 1970s and beyond.

For progressives, history is full of might-have-beens: had Roosevelt lived . . . had Kennedy not been shot . . . had a few thousand hanging chads in Florida not allowed the 2000 election to be stolen . . . had Hillary Clinton been more alert to hacked emails and the need to get out and campaign in Detroit and Milwaukee. But the saddest and most damaging of all was Johnson and Vietnam, which was not a random event but a systemic blunder. It was the Vietnam split and 1968 election that set in motion the serial calamities that followed—the rupture of the progressive governing coalition, the short-circuiting of a biracial, progressive New South, the move of subsequent Democratic presidents to the right, the enshrining of neoliberalism as the dominant ideology, the loss of white working-class voters to Democrats far beyond the dynamics of simple racial backlash, the election of Nixon, the increasingly far-right courts, and the eventual shift of the Republican Party to full-on fascism.

History is filled with such contingent events. Joe Biden, at last, appreciates the power of the New Deal model, the need for a new and durable multiracial governing coalition, and a prudent U.S. stance in the world. Yet the political circumstances could hardly be less auspicious. It will be a long and arduous road back, one that will take luck as well as clarity and conviction.

5

The Great Reversal

In the 1970s, the long half-life of the New Deal system came to an end. The cause was a mash-up of bad luck, bad policy, bad economic theory, and a weak Democratic president. A chart made famous by my colleagues at the Economic Policy Institute shows the growth of the economy and median wages increasing in lockstep every year from 1948 until 1973. Beginning in the late 1970s, those lines diverge and the divergence keeps growing wider; by 2000 the chart looks more like the wide expanse of a shark's mouth from the film *Jaws*.

By 2022, the three wealthiest people had more wealth than the bottom 50 percent. People who made their billons from

The Growing Gap Between Productivity and Pay

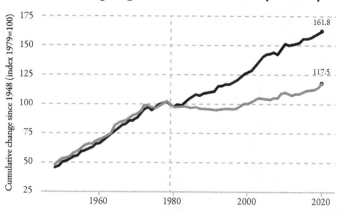

private equity pay little or no taxes. Most ordinary workers have not had a raise (if we adjust for inflation) in forty years. Those trends were all set in motion in the 1970s.

What happened? For a time, as economists looked back on this great reversal, the wrong factors were blamed. It was said that slower growth killed equal prosperity; or that the boomers did it—with the entrance of large numbers of young baby boomers and women into the workforce, it was only natural that less experienced workers would earn less, widening inequality. Some economists also pointed to the increased share of the labor force working in the service sector, which includes rocket scientists at one extreme and fast-food workers at the other, and makes for a less egalitarian income distribution than that of the industrial economy.

But these factors were secondary. The main cause was the destruction of the social contract that had prevailed since the New Deal, in which capital was well regulated, labor was empowered, and government intervened on behalf of the common man and woman.

The immediate precipitating factor was inflation, which hit 12.2 percent in 1974. There was great contention about inflation's causes and cures. By the end of the decade, the wrong analysis and the wrong remedies had prevailed, doing further damage to what was left of the New Deal legacy and its political coalition. Alarm at inflation eventually led the Federal Reserve to pursue the sledgehammer cure of an engineered recession in 1979, doing further damage to worker incomes and bargaining power.

Inflation anxiety also promoted misguided policies of extensive deregulation, in both the financial sector and the rest of the economy, in the vain hope that greater competition would somehow temper prices. Deregulation did the opposite. Combined with the wreckage of antitrust enforcement, it produced greater concentration. These remedies did not address the underlying causes of inflation, but they did help economic elites to shake off the constraints of managed capitalism. The beneficiaries were Ronald Reagan, a half-century of conservative political hegemony, and the entrenchment of neoliberal economics in both parties.

Inflation began ticking upward in the 1960s, initially because Johnson's "guns and butter"—the Vietnam War stimulus plus increased domestic spending and a tax cut—had overheated the economy. This was classic inflation driven by demand. As late as 1965, the inflation rate as measured by the Consumer Price Index was a well-behaved 1.4 percent. By 1969, it was 5.5 percent. Then came the end of the Bretton Woods system in 1973, the devaluation of the dollar, and the first of the two OPEC oil shocks, all of which intensified price pressures.

The Bretton Woods system of fixed exchange rates anchored by the U.S. dollar was living on borrowed time. The dollar was playing the role of global currency, but the global economy was now several times larger than it had been in 1944. The architects of Bretton Woods had tried and failed to get the political leaders to devise some kind of global currency. As early as 1959, a Belgian economist named Robert Triffin warned that the dollar could not be the currency of an expanding world economy without triggering inflation at home. So dollar devaluation would have to come sooner or later.

In those years, dollars could still be exchanged for gold at $35 an ounce. Some foreign leaders, led by Charles de Gaulle of France, who resented America's "exorbitant privilege" of printing the world's dominant currency, began cashing in their dollar holdings for gold, betting on devaluation. Reserves at Fort Knox dwindled. In 1971, in response, Nixon abruptly devalued the dollar and suspended gold convertibility; a cheaper dollar only intensified the inflation. All of this blew up the Bretton Woods currency system, and by 1973 the world shifted to floating exchange rates. Money had become another tradable commodity.

Among the losers of the dollar devaluation were the oil-exporting countries, since oil is denominated in dollars. In October 1973, Egypt and Syria launched a surprise attack on Israel to take back territories lost in the 1967 war, in what became known as the Yom Kippur War. Israeli forces were routed. President Nixon gave Israel $2.2 billion in emergency military aid. At that point, the OPEC countries, led by the Saudis, announced an oil embargo against Israel's allies, with steep production cuts and price hikes. They correctly gambled that Nixon, bogged down in Watergate and a dollar crisis, would not go to war over oil. By the time OPEC lifted the embargo in March 1974, the exporting nations had quadrupled the price of oil to $12 a barrel, pushing inflation into double digits.

But this was no ordinary inflation. It soon became known as stagflation—the simultaneous outbreak of rising inflation and rising unemployment. In standard economics, this could not occur because inflation was supposedly the result of too much demand chasing too little supply, a condition usually associated with tight labor markets. But in the 1970s, the same drag on the economy produced by a quadrupling of oil prices also cut into other purchasing power. It was a supply shock that created a demand shock. This should have been a tipoff that something unusual was at work. Unfortunately, most economists did not grasp that at the time. The supposed trade-off between inflation and unemployment was expressed in a graph called the Phillips curve, loosely associated with Keynesian economists such as Paul Samuelson. Ergo, since stagflation was defying the usual trade-off, it must discredit the entire Keynesian model.

For free-market economists, who had been in disgrace ever since the Great Crash of 1929, stagflation was an ideological windfall. Milton Friedman, who had been a fringe figure, was treated as a seer. Friedman believed that price levels were entirely a function of the money supply, that the Fed should just keep monetary policy on automatic pilot and not adjust interest rates; and by extension the government should keep its hands off the economy entirely.

The 1970s became an era of several variations on Friedman. All boiled down to the idea that markets always get prices right, and invariably work better than governments. Other conservative theorists contended that competition actually worked better without antitrust laws; and that stock markets, by definition, set prices exactly right no matter how much manipulation by insiders. The practical lessons of the 1920s and 1930s, which should have demolished such views for all time, vanished into the national memory hole. But these ideas proved immensely convenient for merger-minded industries and predatory bankers who were more than ready to shake off the shackles of New Deal regulation. And they found a willing ally in President Jimmy Carter.

Political parties seldom get a do-over so soon after a fiasco such as Vietnam, but in 1976 thanks to Watergate the Democratic Party got just that. Unfortunately, Jimmy Carter bungled his opportunity almost as badly as Lyndon Johnson bungled Vietnam. When Carter declared for president on December 12, 1974, his national recognition in the polls was around 2 percent—not his approval rating but people who had heard of him at all. The day he declared, at a National Press Club event, I happened to be the junior reporter on the *Washington Post* national staff and I drew the assignment to cover the announcement. I was the only reporter from a major publication to show up. The *Post* editors cut my story in half, and buried it in the back pages.

Yet Carter, campaigning for almost two years, emerged as the front-runner. By 1976, Vietnam was over, Watergate was over, and the country was eager to move on. Carter had nothing to do with any of that. He was about as far removed from Washington as you could get. He was a total outsider and a novelty—a nuclear engineer and submarine commander who became a peanut farmer, and then a one-term Georgia governor.

Carter ran for the nomination against a weak Democratic field where the liberals, Mo Udall of Arizona and Birch Bayh of Indiana, never caught fire. George Wallace mounted another run for president, this time as a Democrat. But an assassin's attempt on his life in May 1972 left Wallace paralyzed, and he was unable to win a primary. Once Carter won the Iowa precinct caucuses followed by the New Hampshire primary and then defeated Udall in Wisconsin, his bandwagon was unstoppable. But in the general election Carter ran a very weak campaign. Even with a crisis of energy and stagflation incurred on the Republican watch, he only barely defeated the accidental president who had pardoned Nixon, Gerald Ford, winning 50.1 percent of the popular vote.

In the post-Watergate revulsion, Democrats had gained FDR-scale majorities in the 1974 midterm election shortly after Nixon's resignation. Despite Carter's own narrow win, Democrats in Congress held on to these margins in 1976, with Roosevelt-scale margins of 292–143 in the House and 61–38 in the Senate. So Democrats might have been primed to complete the unfinished business of the New Deal and the Great Society.

Except this was not Carter's agenda. Under Carter, no major domestic social or economic legislation was enacted, other than Republican-inspired tax cuts and deregulation, feckless measures for energy conservation, and a modest public works act passed in 1977. Carter was not eager to revive unions, whose power was seen as an instrument of inflation, so he did not use his office to help enact labor law reform. The only important piece of progressive legislation of the Carter presidency, the Humphrey-Hawkins Act of 1978, provided that the Federal Reserve was obligated to promote full employment as well as price stability. It originated entirely in Congress. Carter's main achievement was to sign it.

Carter declared in his January 1978 State of the Union address, "Government cannot solve our problems. It can't set the goals. It cannot define our vision. Government cannot eliminate poverty, or provide a bountiful economy, or reduce inflation, or save our cities, or cure illiteracy, or provide energy." As Arthur Schlesinger Jr. wrote, in the *New Republic*, "If [FDR] had taken Carter's view of government, we still would be in the Great Depression."

Carter's desire to be a centrist good-government president was quickly upstaged by the twin crises of energy and inflation. Oil suffered a supply shock, but it was not the only one. Bad harvests in Russia and other random events had led to global grain shortages and hikes in the price of food. Meanwhile, the enactment of Medicare and Medicaid in 1965, with government paying full-sticker prices imposed by doctors and hospitals (part of the deal to get the law through Congress), led to inflation in the health sector. Rising interest rates raised mortgage costs. As inflation fed on itself, housing became attractive as a shelter against inflation, bidding up housing prices still further. The effects of aggregate demand, wrote Alan Blinder, later vice chair of the Federal Reserve, "were minor compared to the supply shocks." These, in Blinder's description, were "a whole host of special one-shot factors." But the economists advising Carter treated the inflation as overheated demand.

In the 1970s, unions still represented one worker in three, and many contracts in major industries had cost-of-living clauses. So when prices increased, wages followed suit. This was known as the wage-price spiral. Here again, dissenting economists proposed what is known as an incomes policy—a strategy for government to work with industry and labor to damp down the spiral using either tax policies to reward wage restraint or direct wage and price controls. The policy had worked well in Sweden, where labor worked with management to hold down inflationary wage demands that could harm Swedish exports. This whole approach had a suspiciously European "tripartite" flavor, and found no takers in the Carter administration.

Finally came the coup de grâce of a recession engineered by the Federal Reserve. In 1979, after a second round of increases on the price of oil triggered by the Iranian Revolution, inflation soared back into double digits, to 13.3 percent. Carter brought in Paul Volcker as Fed chair, with instructions to do whatever it took to brake price increases. Volcker resolved to end inflation by putting the economy through the wringer of a deep recession.

In October 1979, Volcker began what would be a series of interest rate hikes, which peaked at 20.5 percent. The economy duly collapsed, and with it the Carter presidency. Small businesses, builders, and homebuyers could not get credit, and economic activity went into a sharp contraction. Unemployment reached 11 percent, the worst since the Great Depression. With a high rate of joblessness, wages declined. This was the beginning of a long period of steadily weakening worker power to defend earnings, intensified by Ronald Reagan's assault on unions just a few years later.

One remedy that was tried, in a half-hearted, off-and-on way, was wage and price controls. Richard Nixon, of all people, first imposed them in 1971, even before the first OPEC oil hike. Nixon, as a junior bureaucrat in wartime Washington, had worked for the Office of Price Administration, which was headed by the arch-liberal John Kenneth Galbraith. Nixon came away from the experience with an abiding hatred for government controls. In 1970, with inflation increasing, the Democratic Congress had given the president standby authority to use wage and price controls, over Nixon's objections, and he had vowed not to use them. Yet in mid-1971, anticipating the 1972 election campaign, Nixon was worried about inflation. So as part of the same announcement that devalued the dollar and ended gold convertibility, Nixon announced a ninety-day wage and price freeze, and created a system of controls. Galbraith, writing a year earlier, had proposed just such a freeze.

At the time, inflation was not even that high. What worried some economists was that it was accelerating, as expectations of steeper price hikes became self-fulfilling prophesies. The freeze was to be Phase I, to break the cycle of expectations. Phase II of Nixon's controls involved an elaborate bureaucracy of price-monitoring, under a Council on Wage and Price Stability, and a mix of direct orders and negotiated price restraints.

This was a far cry from the comprehensive system of wage and price controls during World War II, but it did serve to dampen inflationary expectations, according to a study published by three Brookings Institution authors who had had leading roles in the price control effort. Orthodox economists hate price controls, because they violate the cardinal principle of free-market economics—the interplay of supply and demand determining price. But as World War II showed under Franklin Roosevelt, in an economic emergency, competently administered price controls are superior to both runaway inflation driven by shortages and a deliberate recession.

Carter was to the right of Nixon on this issue. Even as inflation spiked into double digits, Carter declared in his January 1978 Message to Congress, "I do not believe in wage and price controls. A sincere commitment to voluntary restraint provides a way, perhaps the only way, to fight inflation without Government interference." This view turned out to be wishful. Ironically, a competent incomes-policy regime could have been a lot better for the economy than the engineered recession to which Carter and Volcker turned in desperation.

In addition to inviting the revival of free-market theory, inflation played havoc with the carefully regulated banking system. As long as there was relative price stability, the system designed by the New Deal could work. Banks and thrift institutions operated in a world of regulated interest rates. Savers could get a decent return. Long-term, fixed-rate loans could deliver a normal profit to lenders.

Banking was usefully boring; a bankers' joke called it the "3-6-3 system": pay depositors 3 percent, lend money at 6 percent, and be on the golf course by 3 p.m. This had wider benefits. Boring banking had relatively well-paid executives, but it did not produce exorbitant profits, salaries, or impenetrable frauds; and it was much easier for government to comprehend and regulate.

Once inflation began ticking upward in the late 1960s, both sides of the banking equation came unstuck. Small depositors, earning low fixed-interest rates on savings accounts and getting no interest on checking accounts, saw their money eroded by inflation. Bankers, meanwhile, were losing money on fixed-rate loans and securities that earned less than the rate of inflation.

The magical cure for all of this, supposedly, was deregulation. In 1972, Merrill Lynch persuaded the SEC to allow it to create a new hybrid called a money market mutual fund. This behaved much like a bank account but paid higher returns that reflected the rising short-term rates in short-term money markets. A few upstart banks got cute and devised a way to pay interest on checking accounts by disguising them as something other than checking accounts. What looked like a check and quacked like a check was rebranded as a Negotiable Order of Withdrawal, in a

NOW account. Regulators soon threw in the towel and allowed all banks to pay interest on checking accounts.

Banks, however, were still getting slammed on both sides of their balance sheets. Depositors were deserting them for money market mutual funds, and they were losing money on fixed-rate loans. Larger corporations, meanwhile, were abandoning bankers and borrowing directly in financial markets by issuing IOUs known as commercial paper. That market increased from $4.5 billion a year in 1960 to $90 billion by 1979.

The commercial bankers looked longingly across the Glass-Steagall wall, where their investment banker cousins were finding new ways to get rich. Under newly indulgent antitrust standards, mergers and acquisitions exploded during this period. The word "conglomerate" was only coined in 1964. In the late 1960s and 1970s, companies with entirely dissimilar lines of business merged. This supposedly produced "synergies." When many of these mergers, heavily reliant on borrowed money, failed to yield the advertised benefits, the same merger and acquisition specialists at the investment banks then underwrote the breakup of the failed conglomerate, making money both ways.

While I was working as chief investigator for the Senate Banking Committee in the mid-1970s, we got regular visits from commercial bankers begging them to be let in on the investment banker action. My boss, Chairman William Proxmire, was sympathetic. So were most governors of the Federal Reserve. The commercial bankers argued to Proxmire and the Fed that investment bankers had a cozy cartel that permitted them captive customers and exorbitant profits. Let commercial bankers do some of that, and the public would benefit from the enhanced competition. As a consumer champion, Proxmire liked that.

What actually occurred once Glass-Steagall was breached was that a few mega-banks, doing both commercial and investment banking, acquired smaller banks and commandeered most of the nation's market share. They in turn resurrected 1920s-style conflicts of interest and concentrated risks based on hidden, "off-balance-sheet" leverage. In 2008, all this opaque leverage crashed the entire financial system.

Long before Glass-Steagall was formally repealed in 1999, exceptions permitted by the Fed and other regulators allowed commercial bankers to underwrite various forms of securities that were technically prohibited, such as municipal bonds, securities backed by commercial paper, or mortgages, or credit card receipts. I was alone among Proxmire's senior staff in being very skeptical, but I later learned that I was in good company. A fellow skeptic was Paul Volcker, then the Fed chairman. Volcker was a fiscal and monetary conservative but also a close student of abuses by bankers. When the Federal Reserve governors in 1987 formally voted, 3 to 2, to allow commercial banks to underwrite several categories of bonds, Volcker was in the minority. A Fed chairman cannot function when he loses control of his board, and Volcker, at just fifty-eight, resigned shortly afterward with six years of his term remaining.

In the indulgent regulatory climate of the Nixon and Carter years, whole new categories of abuses proliferated. The most cheeky was the leveraged buyout. "Leverage" is a polite word for debt. It was one thing to orchestrate a merger with willing partners, another to grab control of a company over the objection of its executives and board. You could do this by borrowing a lot of money, paying a premium price for its shares, and then taking majority control. The borrowed money then became a liability on the balance sheet of the target company, often loading it with crippling debt. This tactic became the signature of the private equity industry that was born in the hostile-takeover movement of the 1970s and 1980s. The financial engineers who cooked up these schemes made their money on the takeover, *whether or not the underlying enterprise failed.* And of course all that additional debt increased the odds of its failure. (See chapter 8.)

Leveraged buyouts began in the late 1960s. The first person to successfully pull off the hostile takeover of a large corporation with borrowed money, against the wishes of its executives and board, was a twenty-nine-year-old nobody named Saul Steinberg. His base of operations was a computer leasing company called Leasco, which had a market value in 1968 of $74 million. Steinberg decided to take over the much larger Reliance Insurance Company, an old-line fire and casualty outfit about ten times Leasco's size. Steinberg coveted Reliance's more than $100 million in excess reserves. Reliance's board rebuffed his overtures. So Steinberg borrowed money, and offered Reliance shareholders a premium over what the stock market was valuing Reliance. He soon got control of the company. Remarkably, though the SEC has substantial authority to prohibit stock market manipulation, the SEC had no problems with Steinberg's gambit.

Once it was clear that such maneuvers were legal, an entire new industry of hostile-takeover artists arose. In the 1970s, an obscure bond trader named Michael Milken at the firm of Drexel Burnham Lambert specialized in bonds of distressed companies, known as "junk bonds." These bonds paid premium interest rates, to compensate for the increased risk. Milken believed that the risk was exaggerated and made a lot of money trading junk bonds. Then he started floating new issues of junk bonds, initially for shaky companies that needed capital, but soon the idea was to use junk bonds to finance hostile takeovers. Large and well-established companies began falling prey to corporate raiders. If the deal went bad, Milken and other junk bond purveyors would provide additional capital with more junk bonds. Many of these companies, loaded up with extensive debt, went broke. Milken eventually went to jail, convicted of insider trading, tax evasion, and stock manipulation.

Even when explicit corruption was not involved, the leveraged buyout turned the normal discipline of capitalism upside down. The traders could get rich regardless of whether or not the underlying enterprise proved viable. It was deemed efficient and good for the economy thanks to two other of the ultra-free-market theories that gained currency in the 1970s and 1980s. One was the argument propounded by Milton Friedman and others that the sole duty of the corporation was to Maximize Shareholder Value. That sounded plausible in theory—after all, the owners of the corporation were the shareholders, not the executives. But in practice, in the context of a hostile takeover the temporary owners (majority shareholders) were the corporate raiders whose main goal was to bid up the price of a stock, cash in, and then dump it later. It was the opposite of responsible stewardship of a corporation.

Despite its invitation to corruption, and the failure of many of the first wave of hostile takeovers, the leveraged buyout was seen by a new generation of free-market theorists as the invisible hand incarnate. An influential Harvard Business School theorist named Michael Jensen argued that since the only duty of corporate owners was to maximize shareholder value, and hostile takeovers were bidding up share prices, then corporate raiders must be doing the hand's work.

Jensen also propounded the "efficient market hypothesis"—the claim that markets always priced goods including securities accurately, notwithstanding the ease with which insiders could manipulate prices. The hypothesis held that whatever markets do is, by definition, efficient. If plain corruption, conflicts of interest, and misleading of investors are at the heart of a scheme, no matter. Markets will somehow ferret that out and price securities "correctly." The financial collapse of 2008 was the definitive proof that insiders could corruptly price financial instruments disastrously wrong, and pawn them off on less well-informed suckers.

Jensen urged that managers should be compensated in stock options, to better align their self-interest with that of shareholders. But it turned out that executives had the ability to manipulate the timing of reported profits, the better to maximize the value of their options. In 2001, after decades of such manipulation, Jensen recanted and declared that paying executives in options was a terrible idea. "It's too easy to game the target-setting process. Nobody has an incentive to provide accurate data or to worry about the company as a whole," he said.

The efficient market theorists left out one real-world detail whose assessment won Joseph Stiglitz the Nobel Prize—the pervasiveness of "information asymmetries" in financial markets. The guy from Goldman who is trying to sell you a bond knows a lot more about it than you do, and can take advantage of that knowledge. The inventors of the efficient market hypothesis had neglected to read their history: exploitation of unequal information destroys the discipline of supply and demand, and is even more of a danger when regulators stop paying attention to conflicts of interest and excess hidden leverage.

The corrupt abuses that led to the collapse of 2008 were close equivalents of the ones that had crashed the economy in 1929. They had been held in abeyance only because of the regulatory schema of the New Deal. When that structure began falling apart in the 1970s, it was only a matter of time before the crash repeated itself.

The resurrected free-market theory did not really drive the policy; raw political power did. But the theory was terrific window dressing and it gave pause to centrist liberals who might have fought back. From the perspective of the traders and speculators who made their billions before the economy collapsed, theorists like Friedman and Jensen were, in a favorite phrase of Joseph Stalin, useful idiots.

Jimmy Carter ushered in deregulation in one other major respect. While the economy was already well on its way toward deregulation of finance, other key industries remained regulated until the late 1970s. The New Deal had regulated airlines, telephones, trucking, natural gas, electricity, and public utilities generally. Some industries, such as telephones, were allowed to be monopolies, but with rates and profits regulated. Others, such as airlines, had multiple carriers, but their routes and fares were also regulated; the premise was that they would compete for market share based on service. Still others, such as electric power, were regulated on the premise that they were natural monopolies (why string two parallel sets of wires?) that also had network efficiencies and economies of scale. Carter, persuaded that deregulation could counter inflation, sponsored policies in 1978 to deregulate all these industries.

In theory, monopolies, even well-regulated ones, can retard innovation. But in my 1996 book, *Everything for Sale*, I extensively studied the historical relationship between regulation and innovation. I found that in most regulated industries, regulation of prices and profits actually promoted innovation and thus greater efficiency, and led to declining prices over time.

Take the case of electric power. If a regulated power company has a specified rate of return on equity set by the government, how does it increase its profits? There is only one way—it must expand its customer base. By innovating and making electricity cheaper, it can increase the pool of customers who can afford it. This is exactly what the power companies did. I found that if you adjust for the cost of fuel, the retail price of electricity declined faster before deregulation than after.

In principle, deregulation permitted end users to shop around for suppliers. In practice, deregulation led to increased market concentration and monopoly pricing power.

The airlines are a similar story. Before 1978, their fares and routes had to be approved by the now defunct Civil Aeronautics Board. Critics argued that new competitors were eager to enter the market, but were kept out by a cozy cartel blessed by the CAB. After 1978, however, when several upstart airlines with names like People Express and New York Air entered the skies, all were crushed within a few years by the major carriers, who could use selective pricing power to offer deep discounts on routes offered by the new competitors. One such special fare was coded FU, just to be sure the challenger got the message. (After more than three decades of chaos, two new airlines, JetBlue and Southwest, did manage to survive and hold on to some market share.)

As in electric power, actual average fares actually fell faster before deregulation. They declined at an annual rate of 2.5 percent adjusted for inflation in the years between 1950 and 1978, but only 1.7 percent between 1978 and 1994. The predictability of a specified rate of return allowed the airlines to invest in new generations of fuel-efficient planes, which were the main source of greater efficiency and declining fares over time. With deregulation, the airlines oscillated between trying to maintain a price cartel and not being able to count on reliable profits. They compensated by reducing their investment in more modern planes, and the fleet got older every year. To increase their pricing power at "fortress hubs," the airlines scheduled relatively fewer non-stops, adding to inefficiency and traveler inconvenience. They also manipulated fares to be sure that every flight would be full. That meant there was no slack in the system, and cascading weather delays could lead to near collapse. None of this occurred under regulation.

By 2010, every major airline had gone bankrupt at least once. There were some bargains to be had, but the free-market model meant that every seat in principle had an infinite number of prices. Some consumers got good deals; those who had to change plans got gouged. And without guaranteed routes and rates of return, the airlines cut service to small cities and maintained monopolies that charged astronomical fares. This in turn had a seriously negative effect on the economic development of many small metro areas.

The story of telephone deregulation was more of a mixed bag. The breakup of the old AT&T monopoly did produce innovation. But deregulation also produced market concentration and price gouging, with just two companies today that produce most cell phones and three that provide most network service.

Regulation of major industries, while it lasted, had important benefits for labor. If a power company or an airline must function with a regulated rate of return, it gains nothing by trying to batter down wages. Its lower labor costs simply produce a different balance sheet but the same rate of return. Since there was nothing to be gained by trashing labor, executives of major industries opted for decently paid and well-trained workers. Not coincidentally, industries such as airlines, telephones, and public utilities had strong and effective unions.

Because unions value equity as an end in itself, they also worked to narrow wage differentials within a company. For example, the International Association of Machinists represents both skilled airline mechanics and relatively unskilled baggage handlers. During the era of regulation, baggage handlers had good pay and job security. After deregulation, airlines had every incentive to increase profits by weakening labor. A lot of baggage handler work was outsourced. Some maintenance was done offshore to take advantage of cheaper labor. The same casualization of work occurred in telephones, electric power, gas pipelines, and trucking. So deregulation generally was a major contributor to the weakening of unions and the undermining of wages and job security. If there were offsetting benefits to consumers, the deregulators might have a stronger case. But consumers have suffered along with workers.

A major player in Carter's deregulation misadventure was a Cornell economist named Alfred Kahn, who became Carter's chair of the Civil Aeronautics Board (CAB) and his adviser on deregulation generally. Kahn later had serious regrets. He wrote that he did not anticipate the abusive industry practices and the pricing power that came with the concentration wrought by deregulation. In a case of poetic justice, deregulated airlines quickly jacked up fares and reduced service on less profitable small-city routes, one of which was Ithaca to Washington, DC.

In that era, even some liberals who were otherwise in favor of a well-regulated form of capitalism, notably Ted Kennedy and Ralph Nader, believed that some regulatory agencies such as the CAB had become hopelessly captive to the industries they regulated, and supported deregulation as the remedy. Both also later expressed regrets and severe criticism of the way deregulation was carried out in practice.

By 1979, Carter was besieged on multiple fronts. Inflation was out of control, and the gas lines of 1974 had returned. The Shah of Iran, long a U.S. puppet, had been overthrown. U.S. policymakers who defended the unpopular Shah to the end were caught off guard. Carter ignored warnings, and American diplomats in Teheran were taken hostage, creating a new crisis.

Over the July 4th weekend, Carter repaired to Camp David for what became ten days to work on a speech about energy. He soon junked that speech and composed a much more lugubrious thirty-three-minute address about America's crisis of confidence. Though he did not use the word "malaise," it soon became known as Carter's malaise speech. It seemed as if he was projecting his own sense of gloom onto the American people. His ratings in the polls rose briefly, but two days later Carter impulsively fired his entire cabinet, leaving people wondering if he had taken leave of his senses. That was the beginning of the end of his presidency.

With Nixon disgraced and a huge Democratic majority in Congress, liberals had hoped for a revival of something like the Great Society. Instead, Carter was governing more like Eisenhower. Going into the 1980 election, Carter looked like a sure loser. At length, the liberals prevailed on Ted Kennedy to challenge Carter in the Democratic primaries. Kennedy agreed, but was ambivalent. When CBS interviewer Roger Mudd asked Kennedy why he wanted to be president, he could not come up with an answer. After a series of bruising primaries, in which Carter beat Kennedy in twenty-four out of thirty-four states, Carter was re-nominated. But the party was as badly divided and dispirited as in 1968, and Carter's stiff, high-minded pessimism was no match for the sunny optimism of Ronald Reagan.

Not only did Carter lose badly—carrying only six states and the District of Columbia and losing the popular vote by nearly ten points—but he took down the Democratic Senate with him. Republicans picked up twelve seats, ending a fifty-year era of Democratic control of the Senate that had survived as a bulwark against three Republican presidencies, except for two brief two-year interludes in 1947–49 and 1953–55. Among the losses were such great progressives as Frank Church, Birch Bayh, George McGovern, Gaylord Nelson, and Warren Magnuson.

As Harry Truman had famously warned, embracing Republican policies was no survival strategy for Democrats—voters would choose the original rather than the copy. The election of Reagan and a Republican Senate ushered in an era every bit as self-reinforcing and durable as the Roosevelt era, with the added advantage that the core Democratic fortress of the labor movement would be steadily weakened, and most economists had become paladins of the free market. Not until practice discredited bad theory would progressivism get another turn. But by the time Democratic politicians and their economic advisers came to terms with new realities, Republican leaders and voters were denying reality altogether.

As this book suggests, the Democrats' serial failures were not dictated either by events or by politics. Johnson did not have to escalate the Vietnam War. Carter did not have to embrace deregulation. Clinton did not have to champion Wall Street speculation, NAFTA, and budget balance. Obama did not have to double down on corporate globalism. These missteps, distancing the Democrats from the New Deal and the common people, were opportunistic and optional. Some of them seemed to make tactical sense at the time, but they were long-term strategic disasters, setting the stage for neo-fascism and Trump.

6

Bad Economics, Worse Politics

The year 1980 seemed to signal a watershed—the end of the era of effective, reliable government. Public management of the economy had faltered. Tax-and-spend had evidently reached its limits. Citizens were rebelling against the taxes, and the spending was not solving the economic frustrations of most citizens.* The public faces of the party leadership reinforced conventional assumptions: Carter was associated with pessimism, rationing, and sweaters. For Reagan it was morning in America, and the new morning was a conservative one. For many commentators and for some stunned Democrats, the challenge of the party of Roosevelt was to find an alternative to New Deal liberalism, in effect to become more like Republicans.

The party's 1984 nominee, Walter Mondale, personified the strategic fallacy of disavowing the Roosevelt-Truman tradition. All his political life, Mondale had been a mainstream liberal. Carter had put him on the ticket in 1976 precisely to reassure the

---

* California's Proposition 13, approved by a margin of nearly 2 to 1 in June 1978, was widely taken as a revolt against big government. It was actually a revolt against a grossly unfair tax system and the failure of the political establishment to prevent housing inflation from raising property assessments and taxing people out of their homes. See the author's *Revolt of the Haves* (New York: Simon and Schuster, 1980).

party's liberal wing. But now, Mondale ran a campaign literally based on apologizing for the Democrats' liberal sins.

His speech to the 1984 Democratic National Convention accepting the party's nomination had to be one of the most self-defeating in party history. Mondale virtually accepted the Republicans' indictment of Democrats as big spenders who were soft on defense, and went on to repudiate the party's core beliefs:

> I want to say something to those of you across the country who voted for Mr. Reagan—to Republicans, to independents, and yes, to Democrats: I heard you. And our party heard you. After we lost, we didn't tell the American people that they were wrong. Instead, we began asking what our mistakes had been.

Apparently, the Democrats' prime mistake had been their liberalism. Mondale continued, "Look at our platform. There are no defense cuts that weaken our security; no business taxes that weaken our economy; no laundry lists that raid our treasury."

Reflect for a moment on the message Mondale was conveying. Military spending—whether Johnson's Vietnam debacle or Reagan's excessive buildup—was sacrosanct; the Democrats' failure had been to spend too little. The entire New Deal model of public outlays to benefit ordinary men and women (still far from complete) was dismissed as a mere "laundry list" of "treasury raids." Mondale was also endorsing the supply-side myth that taxing corporations or banks was bad for the economy.

In this speech, Mondale was conceding the entire Republican caricature of Democrats. Had the Republican National Committee written Mondale's talking points, it could hardly have done better. Obviously, there was no way Mondale was going to out-Reagan Reagan—on taxes, domestic spending cuts, or military spending. His acceptance speech might as well have been a concession speech.

And it got worse. Mondale proposed increasing taxes, but solely for the purpose of budget balance. This was the beginning of a syndrome in which Democrats watched Republicans increase the federal deficit by cutting taxes and hiking military outlays, sometimes even joining them—and then took on the thankless role of the fiscal grown-ups in the room, calling for tax increases and further domestic spending cuts purely for fiscal discipline. It was the least politically attractive part of the New Deal model—the taxes without the valued spending. And having sworn off higher taxes on business as bad for the economy, the Democrats ended up supporting regressive taxes on working people or cuts in social outlays as part of bipartisan budget deals.

In this same acceptance speech, Mondale's prime criticism of Reagan was that he had increased deficits, as if fiscal rectitude were the issue most on the minds of voters suffering from stagnant living standards. Mondale vowed:

> Whoever is inaugurated in January, the American people will have to pay Mr. Reagan's bills. The budget will be squeezed. Taxes will go up. By the end of my first term, I will reduce the Reagan Budget deficit by two-thirds. Let's tell the truth. It must be done, it must be done. Mr. Reagan will raise taxes, and so will I. He won't tell you. I just did.

The architect of this politics was Robert Rubin, the co-CEO of Goldman Sachs, who began as a Mondale money raiser and soon became a key policy adviser. Mondale's strategists hoped that his budgetary candor would earn respect. But his stance as fiscal scold and repudiator of the New Deal tradition did not thrill voters in November. Reagan carried forty-nine states.

The contrast between the Democrats' slide from FDR to

Carter to Mondale and the Republicans' Goldwater-Nixon-Reagan odyssey is striking. In the sixteen years between Goldwater's crushing defeat in 1964 and Reagan's epic victory in 1980, Republicans did not endeavor to become more like Democrats. They developed a compelling, modernized conservative worldview of their own. Democrats had to spend more than half a century wandering in their confused wilderness before finding their way back to a convincing progressivism in 2021.

Mondale's self-annihilating 1984 campaign was part of a climate of Democratic and liberal remorse and revisionism. His prime opponent for the nomination was Colorado senator Gary Hart, not a Roosevelt progressive but a techno-futurist. Hart spoke relentlessly of "new ideas." A telling put-down of Hart was a cartoon by Dan Wasserman in which Hart says, "America needs new ideas." A citizen asks him to name one, and Hart responds, "I just did!" In a debate with Hart, Mondale famously invoked a Wendy's ad, telling Hart, "When I hear your call for new ideas, I'm reminded of that commercial, 'Where's the beef?'"

But both Hart and Mondale, despite their ostensible differences, each expressed versions of the same broad assumption that something was fatally wrong with the New Deal model. Mondale's strategy was to embrace much of the Republican critique; Hart's was to be post-ideological and technological. Neither stance was convincing to voters.

In the 1980s, the quest for a different brand of Democrat was in the air. It could be seen in the media, in several party organs, in intellectual revisionism, and in the increasing Democratic alliance with corporate money and with Wall Street.

An influential book of the era was titled *The End of Liberalism*. The 1969 book, by the Cornell political scientist Theodore Lowi, criticized the evolution of the broad programs of the New Deal era into what Lowi disparaged as "interest-group liberalism." Rather than government benefiting the collectivity, Lowi argued, liberalism had become mere "clientelism."

The free-market economists' version of the same argument, called public choice theory, held that government was hopelessly inefficient and corrupt because of the logic of "rent seeking"*— using political influence to get funding for special causes. According to the theory, interest groups in bed with their political patrons and bureaucratic allies raided the public treasury. Funds went not to the most deserving but the most politically connected, which was inefficient economically. The market, by contrast, allocated resources fairly and rationally.

Ironically, if you look at public choice theory from the perspective of the years after 1980, it nicely describes the corrupt relationship between financiers and their allies in government who dismantled salutary regulation, so that bankers and traders could pursue rents with impunity. The most potent interest group of all was Wall Street. Compared to Goldman Sachs, even the AARP was a minor player.

Curiously, the maligned interest groups in public choice theory included trade unionists seeking a living wage, elderly people pursuing adequate pensions and medical care, and Black citizens calling on government to complete the unfinished promise of civil rights. But the most quietly influential interest group of them all was seldom included in the analysis, because financial markets were said to be efficient by definition. Wall Street's role as a political powerhouse in making self-serving rules of capitalism was simply ignored. And in the 1980s and 1990s, Wall Street became increasingly influential among Democrats as well as Republicans.

---

* "Rent" is the economist's term for excess profits. James Buchanan redefined it to mean unearned social outlays.

Public choice theory won a Nobel for one of its inventors, a previously obscure Virginia economist named James Buchanan. As if to prove Buchanan's point of political corruption, the Nobel itself became highly politicized in that era. A former Swedish social democrat who had migrated far to the right, named Assar Lindbeck, became the power player on the Nobel committee. He made sure that the Nobel in economics would be bestowed on market fundamentalists like Buchanan and Milton Friedman. The free marketplace of ideas is one more market that doesn't work like the model.

Ironically, Lowi considered himself a man of the liberal left. His actual writing was much more subtle than the widely quoted one-liner. His work resonated with the earlier left-wing critique of pluralism, which pointed out that in a grossly unequal society the rich exerted disproportionate influence. Lowi campaigned for the progressive challenger Eugene McCarthy in 1968. But "interest-group liberalism" became an all-purpose put-down of the Democrats' coalition politics, echoed by the era's neoliberal intellectuals such as Bill Galston and Elaine Kamarck of the Democratic Leadership Council.

Many moderate-to-liberal economists of that era, who might have been Keynesians at an earlier time, became newly enamored of the claims of the efficiency of free markets. They cheered on the deregulation begun under Carter and intensified under Reagan. They became crusaders for a deeper brand of grand of globalization, and critics of deficits to finance social spending. The Brookings Institution Democrat Alice Rivlin, the first director of the newly created Congressional Budget Office (1975–83) and later director of the Office of Management and Budget, became a relentless deficit hawk in the Clinton White House.

The same ideological revisionism was reflected in the media of that era. It all reinforced the new conventional wisdom:

the trouble with liberals was their liberalism. The *New Republic*, once a proud voice of American progressivism, made a sharp turn to the right after it was bought by Martin Peretz in 1974. In addition to continuing to publish some liberals like Hendrick Hertzberg and me, *TNR* began regularly featuring leading conservatives of the day such as Fred Barnes, Morton Kondracke, Charles Krauthammer, and later Andrew Sullivan.

Peretz, having been part of the New Left in the 1960s, renounced his youthful views. He also became a passionate Zionist. His views on Israel put him in league with Democrats and Republicans who were not only strongly pro-Israel but conservative on defense generally. The magazine supported Reagan's aid to the Nicaraguan Contras, the Gulf War, and the Iraq War. Its hawkishness often led *TNR* to be scornful of liberalism across the board, since liberals tended to be critics of military excess and sympathetic to the aspirations of the third world, even including (God forbid) Palestine.

TNR was close to the Democratic Leadership Council. Hedge fund operator Michael Steinhardt, the principal financial backer of the DLC in its early years, was later Peretz's co-owner. In 2004, *TNR* endorsed DLC stalwart Joe Lieberman for president. The *New Republic* and the DLC often favored the same policies, and *TNR* frequently published DLC intellectuals.

TNR also delighted in contrarianism, invariably at the expense of liberalism. An emblematic cover story of the era was headlined "Greedy Geezers," arguing that senior citizens had it too good, thanks to Social Security and Medicare. The article waltzed around the fact that without Social Security, whose median monthly benefit was well below $1,000, more than half of the elderly would have been in poverty. It published an error-ridden cover story by conservative Betsy McCaughey attacking the Hillary Clinton health plan, as well as a ten-thousand-word piece by the well-subsidized neo-con intellectual Charles Murray blaming poverty on the poor.

Yet *TNR* retained the prestige of years past as a flagship liberal journal. It also thrived on the sheer wit of marquee writers such as Hertzberg and Michael Kinsley. Few readers were aware that its repositioning was mainly the result of the philosophical life crisis of its publisher. Rather, the magazine's rejection of liberalism was taken as part of a new, smart zeitgeist. When I worked at *TNR*, the phrase "even the *New Republic*" became an oft-repeated cliché invoked by mainstream and conservative commentators to justify successive lurches to the right. If "even the *New Republic*," the very citadel of liberalism, was for cuts in Social Security . . . privatized Medicare . . . weaker unions . . . you name it, there must be something to the argument.

A new journal, the *Washington Monthly*, founded in 1969, tried to fashion a liberalism that relied less on government. Charles Peters, the magazine's founder and editor, appropriated the term "neoliberalism" to mean a less bureaucratic brand of liberalism that reinvigorated citizenship. The *Monthly*, unlike the snarky *New Republic*, was at least idealistic and warmhearted. But in the course of looking for a liberalism that didn't involve the state, the *Monthly* became part of the chorus of government-bashing.

In 1986, when five colleagues and I founded the Economic Policy Institute (EPI),* there simply was no mainstream research institute challenging the conventional thinking on economics. Brookings, a centrist operation with a lot of business funding,

---

* The others were Ray Marshall, Lester Thurow, Robert Reich, Barry Bluestone, and Jeff Faux.

was typically and mistakenly referred to by the media as a liberal think tank.

We approached the labor movement for seed funding, and got EPI up and running with an initial budget of $1.3 million from nine unions. Over the years, some foundations began gingerly supporting EPI; and it produced very influential research products on widening income inequality and its causes; detailed annual almanacs titled *The State of Working America*; critiques of supply-side assumptions about taxes, investment, and growth, and a great deal more. EPI became a post-graduate school for respected dissenting economists. Its work was always empirical; and because it was challenging the conventional wisdom, EPI was scrupulously careful not to make mistakes. Several EPI alums went into the Biden administration—notably Jared Bernstein and Heather Boushey to the Council of Economic Advisers, and Thea Lee and Janelle Jones to subcabinet posts at the Labor Department.

EPI has succeeded in helping to change the conventional policy wisdom on everything from unemployment and inflation to trade, industrial policy, and budget balance. EPI's extensive work on the relationship between skills and earnings altered the standard thinking in the economics progression, which tended to blame increasing inequality on widening skills differentials rather than widening power differentials.

After long serving as a voice in the wilderness, EPI's general stance on economic issues now informs that of the Biden administration. But this is very much a David and Goliath story. For most of its existence, EPI's budget has been under $5 million a year, and until very recently it was seen as a somewhat risky grantee for mainstream foundations. Right-wing think tanks, meanwhile, raise huge sums. The Heritage Foundation has an annual budget of about $125 million. The American Enterprise Institute spends over $50 million a year. Both have assets of over

$300 million. More centrist-liberal think tanks, such as the Center on Budget and Policy Priorities, that address poverty but are not close to the labor movement and do not challenge the fundamental structures of American capitalism are able to raise in excess of $50 million a year. Robert Rubin has been a keynote speaker at CBPP fundraising events.

Once again, the invisible hand places a thumb on the scale of ideological and political discourse. Views that reinforce the claimed virtue of the wealthy and the powerful get all the money they need. More adversarial views have to scramble. I got a close-up view of just how this worked when I was invited to participate in a luncheon debate at the Philanthropy Roundtable, the association of right-wing funders. The idea was that I would debate one of the leading neo-conservative intellectuals, William Kristol. I accepted, with the proviso that I be allowed to stay for the afternoon session. That afternoon panel was made up of the heads of the top right-wing think tanks, Heritage, Cato, AEI, and the Manhattan Institute. They explained, gratefully, how the major conservative foundations gave them very long-term general funding in the tens of millions because of an alignment of strategic purpose.

I could only reflect on my own experience raising small sums for the *Prospect* and EPI from risk-averse program officers, looking over their shoulders at more centrist foundation presidents and corporate-dominated boards. Our grants tended to be mostly for one year, in the low six figures if that, and the subject of endless haggling. Few center-left foundations shared the conservatives' strategic sense of investing in core progressive infrastructure for the long term.* That began to change around

---

* Three happy exceptions were Ford and MacArthur, which did give the *Prospect* multi-year six-figure grants in its early years, and the Schumann Foundation, headed by Bill Moyers, who has been a mainstay.

2010, but the groups that got the major funding tended to be center-left rather than progressive, Exhibit A being the Center for American Progress, which was widely viewed as the Clinton government in exile, awaiting the election of the next Clinton. Only lately have some large foundations become bolder and more explicitly and strategically progressive.

In 1989, Bob Reich, Paul Starr, and I founded the *American Prospect*. We were all refugees from the *New Republic*. In those years, *The Nation* magazine stood for the far left, and the *New Republic* was neoliberal. Between those two was an ideological chasm wide enough for the entire mainstream progressive tradition. Our reasoning with the *Prospect* was similar to the rationale for EPI. The Democrats had just lost the third presidential election in a row. The absence of a serious magazine or think tank making the case for a mainstream politics in the New Deal–Great Society tradition was adding to the right-wing undertow.

We organized the magazine as an alliance of journalists who brought a deeper analysis than the day's headlines, and scholars who could write for a broad audience. When we launched the first issue in the spring of 1990, we got respectful notices, but several reviewers were puzzled that we were not just another species of "neo," apologizing for traditional liberalism. Over the years we've had some influence helping to reclaim and rekindle a politically viable progressivism, and have launched the careers of many leading progressive journalists through our Young Writing Fellows Program. As with EPI, keeping the *Prospect* solvent has been a constant challenge.

Ironically, both Paul Starr and Bob Reich went to work for Bill Clinton. Paul took a one-year leave from Princeton and helped design Clinton's abortive health plan, which subsequently had great influence on the design of Obama's Affordable Care Act. Bob became labor secretary in Clinton's first term, less as an ideological soul mate and more as a longtime Friend of Bill. Bob, who was less radical himself in those years, served valiantly as one of a handful of token progressives in a neoliberal administration.

In the Democrats' slide to the center, two major party organs connected ideological revisionism and corporate money: the Democratic Congressional Campaign Committee and the Democratic Leadership Council. The DCCC is the fundraising arm of the House Democratic Caucus. Its purpose had mainly been to help reelect incumbents, and it was a very modest player until an obscure Fresno congressman named Tony Coelho became its chair in 1981. In the previous cycle, covering 1979–80, the DCCC had raised just $1.8 million, not much more than its own costs, and only about one-tenth what the Republican counterpart raised. In 1981, Coelho was well positioned to raise money from the corporate political action committees for House Democrats. Reagan had just been elected, his top priority was a massive tax cut. Republicans controlled the Senate but Democrats still controlled the House.

Coelho's strategy was to raise lots of corporate money on the premise that corporations needed Democrats to be their allies. This strategy increased DCCC funding nearly tenfold, to $15 million by 1985–86. In the 1983–84 cycle, the corporate PACs actually gave Democrats more money than they gave Republicans. When I interviewed Rep. Pat Williams, a Montana progressive, about Coelho, he told me on the record that Coelho sometimes arranged to delay House roll call votes because they coincided with DCCC fundraising events.

(Coelho prefigured another corporate Democrat, Rahm Emanuel, who headed the DCCC from 2005 to 2009. One strategy of Emanuel's was to more than double the size of the House Financial Services Committee, so that he could load it up with center-right Democrats who could use their influence on the committee to raise large sums from Wall Street. In 2010, when the committee's liberal chairman, Barney Frank, was trying to get a strong version of what became the Dodd-Frank bill reported to the House floor, there were times when he lacked a working majority on his own committee.)

While Coelho was cashing in on the willingness of Democrats to cast votes more favorable to business, Reagan was demolishing what remained of House Democrats' resistance to a massive and regressive tax cut. The 1981 Economic Recovery Tax Act cut individual tax rates by 23 percent, and reduced corporate rates by liberalizing depreciation allowances. As late as mid-July, Democrats had the votes to block the bill on the House floor. But Democrats sensed which way the political winds were blowing and wanted to share in the credit. The Democratic House Ways and Means Committee chairman, Dan Rostenkowski, began by proposing a modest tax cut more directed at the middle class. When that didn't fly, he ended up co-sponsoring Reagan's bill, and the game was over. By July 29, the administration bill passed the House 323 to 107, with a majority of Democrats voting in favor. Democrats were literally in a bidding war with Republicans to lard up the bill with special interest provisions so that they could share in the credit. Gregg Easterbrook, writing in *The Atlantic*, aptly termed the tax episode combined with the Coelho operation as the time "the party tried to sell its soul and failed."

After Mondale's epic defeat in 1984, centrist Democrats urging a more conservative Democratic Party created the Democratic Leadership Council. The organizers of the DLC were mainly Southern governors and senators who viewed the party's lingering liberalism on race and other social issues as poison in their region. They were in league with corporate Democrats who felt that a more conservative party had both electoral and self-serving advantages. The DLC thus had no difficulty raising plenty of business money. These politicians were joined by some anti-liberal intellectuals. The matchmaker for the DLC partnership was an ambitious former congressional staffer for Rep. Gillis Long of Louisiana named Al From, who had also worked at the Carter White House. The DLC coined the label "New Democrats," as distinguished from presumably bad "old Democrats."

As he tells the story in his memoir, From recruited Bill Clinton to chair the DLC, and then run for president.

> A little after four o'clock on the afternoon of April 6, 1989, I walked into the office of Governor Bill Clinton on the second floor of the Arkansas State Capitol in Little Rock. "I've got a deal for you," I told Clinton after a few minutes of political chit-chat. "If you agree to become chairman of the DLC, we'll pay for your travel around the country, we'll work together on an agenda, and I think you'll be president one day and we'll both be important." With that proposition, Clinton agreed to become chairman of the Democratic Leadership Council, and our partnership was born.

Just to seal the deal, Al From offered Clinton a salary of $100,000 a year, a nice raise from his pay of $35,000 as governor of Arkansas. After Clinton won the election, he returned the favor to the DLC by throwing a massive fundraising event in December 1992. The event took over Union Station, where tables went for $15,000 each. Some 139 trade associations, lobbyists, law firms, and corporations donated over $3.3 million to the DLC in a single evening. With an ally in the White House, the budget of the DLC and its affiliated think tank, the Progressive Policy Institute, reached about $7 million by the end of the Clinton presidency.

Other leaders of the DLC included center-right, mostly Southern governors and senators such as Chuck Robb of Virginia, Sam Nunn of Georgia, who was the DLC's founding chair, Florida's Bob Graham, and Tennessee's Jim Sasser and Al Gore. These states still elected moderate Democrats, but they walked a political tightrope with white Southern voters. Republican opponents regularly used the liberal reputation of the national Democratic Party against them. Jesse Jackson's run for the Democratic nomination in 1988 only intensified the problem. A more centrist national party would be less toxic for centrist Southern politicians.

Despite the DLC's success in repositioning the national party to the center under Clinton in the 1990s, it didn't save centrist Southern Democrats. The number of moderate Senate Democrats representing Southern states* dwindled from eight in 1996, to three in 2006, two in 2014, and zero in 2018. Not until Georgia elected two unrepentant progressives in 2020, relying on a very different appeal, ideology, and coalition, did Southern Democrats return to the Senate.

In a DLC manifesto written in 1989, titled "The Politics of Evasion," William Galston and Elaine Kamarck excoriated progressives for the sin of Liberal Fundamentalism: "Since the late 1960s, the public has come to associate liberalism with tax and spending policies that contradict the interests of average families; with welfare policies that foster dependence rather than self-reliance; with softness toward the perpetrators of crime and indifference toward its victims; with ambivalence toward the assertion of American values and interests abroad; and with an adversarial stance toward mainstream moral and cultural values." That critique sounded plausible, until you realized that both Carter in 1980 and Mondale in 1984 had fled their liberalism as fast as was decently possible, and it didn't save them.

---

* Not counting Virginia, where the fast-growing and liberal DC suburbs have transformed its political composition. Alabama anomalously elected a moderate Democrat, Doug Jones, in 2017 to serve out the unfinished two-year term of Jeff Sessions; Republicans had nominated a discredited far-right candidate in Roy Moore. Jones was handily defeated in 2020.

The DLC critique called for toning down Democratic support for affirmative action, being tougher on crime, joining Republicans in backing tax cuts and deregulation, and moving away from the alliance with trade unions. Instead the idea was to serve the interests of the broad middle class. But how? In a capitalist economy that is growing more rapacious by the year thanks to deregulation, there is simply no substitute for broad or universal programs such as Social Security, regulations that contain the abuses of capital and empower regular people as workers and citizens, and unions as a counterweight to corporations.

It fell to Bill Clinton to translate that ideology into a program. Clinton's campaign for president positioned him as a New Democrat, reinforcing the view that there was something fatally wrong with old Democrats. Carter and Mondale had both attempted this and failed, but Clinton was a much more agile politician. Clinton also had the advantage of running against George H.W. Bush, after twelve years of Republican rule; and Bush was a far less effective politician than Reagan.

The 1992 election had the further oddity of a highly visible third-party candidate, H. Ross Perot. The Perot campaign was a jumble of anti-system themes, including the threat of job losses to Mexico ("a giant sucking sound") and a weird obsession with the budget deficit. Perot, in a more populist version of Mondale's fiscal alarmism, turned the rising national debt into an emblem of the bipartisan failure of the political establishment. Such was the mistrust of politicians as usual that at one point in the spring of 1992, Perot was running ahead of both Bush and Clinton in the polls.

There was a disconnect between Perot's program and what was actually troubling voters, but Perot stood for the revulsion against politics as usual. Does that ring a bell? Fully twenty-four years before Donald Trump was elected president, a made-for-TV protest candidate whose persona and themes did not add up to a coherent governing program was a very serious contender *as a pseudo-populist billionaire*. Such was public disaffection from politics as usual. So Trump was an accident waiting to happen. It only took a perfect storm of events in 2016 for such a protest candidate to get elected. Trump, of course, won the nomination of a major party; Perot as an independent got 19 percent in a three-way race, allowing Clinton to be elected with 43 percent.

Clinton's campaign was a mash-up of a conspicuous right-wing shift on social issues initially combined with traditional Democratic economic themes. A fresh memory was the savaging of Michael Dukakis for having sponsored a work release program that had allowed the release of Willie Horton, who then committed a rape. In his shift to the right on social issues, Clinton went out of his way to disparage a radical Black rapper named Sister Souljah at a conference convened by Jesse Jackson. Clinton made a special trip back to Little Rock so that he could approve the execution of a mentally impaired convict named Ricky Ray Rector. Yet as the famous sign in Clinton headquarters reminded campaign workers, "The Economy, Stupid," economic themes were paramount. In his standard campaign speech, Clinton declared, "One percent of Americans at the top of the totem pole now have more wealth than the bottom 90 percent." And he often added, all too accurately, that we were in danger of raising "the first generation of Americans to do worse than their parents."

Once in office, however, Clinton's remedies were mainly New Democrat. A big article of faith was the importance of job training, a weak nostrum for inequality vigorously promoted (and later disavowed) by Robert Reich. Clinton became a passionate free trader, and gratuitously embraced NAFTA, an unfinished creation of George H.W. Bush. Meanwhile, on the social front, Clinton flipped back to liberal and managed to achieve some incremental progress while offending just about everyone with his gays-in-the-military policy of "don't ask, don't tell." Conservatives were outraged that he ended the ban on gays serving, and gays were appalled at the premise that they had something to be ashamed of. Clinton repeatedly raised the idea of cutting or partly privatizing Social Security as part of a grand bargain on budget balance (a project relentlessly promoted by Robert Rubin), and had to be regularly talked out of it by his political advisers.

Clinton's first two years were a debacle. His health plan, the complex public-private creation of a task force headed by Hillary Clinton, neglected to enlist key congressional leaders in its design. It was dead on arrival on Capitol Hill, and never even came to a vote. Clinton spent enormous political capital on NAFTA, which was opposed by about two-thirds of the House Democratic Caucus. When NAFTA finally passed, it was mainly with Republican House support, and leaving in its wake great bitterness and a divided Democratic Party. These splits going into the 1994 midterm election led to the loss of fifty-three Democratic House seats and the installation of Newt Gingrich as Speaker.

Once he lost his congressional majority, Clinton moved further to the right, relying on two DLC-affiliated pollster-strategists, Mark Penn and Douglas Schoen, who came up with the strategy known as "triangulation." The idea was to put the president above party—his own party as well as the opposition party. With Republican votes and Democratic opposition, Clinton carried out his campaign pledge to "end welfare as we know it," substituting a stingy replacement for Aid to Families with Dependent Children that left millions of needy people in poverty without providing the promised ladders to a better life through work and childcare.

Throughout his presidency and in his influence beyond it, Clinton was a Typhoid Mary figure. He survived; those around him got sick.

One of Clinton's most perverse and enduring legacies was the worship of budget balance. It became an article of faith for two generations of Democratic economists and the candidates and presidents they influenced. The obsession with deficit reduction was partly a product of Clinton having to run against Ross Perot, but it mostly reflected the influence of Fed Chair Alan Greenspan as seconded by Rubin.

When Greenspan first met President-Elect Clinton, on December 3, 1992, in Little Rock, the Fed chairman gave Clinton a tutorial on deficits, interest rates, and inflation. As Greenspan explained it, the Fed controlled short-term rates, but long-term rates were set by supply and demand in the bond market. Long-term rates were currently too high, because money markets were worried that a large deficit portended rising inflation. With high inflation, an investor needed a higher rate of return on a long-term bond or a mortgage in order to offset the declining real value of principal. Therefore, if you want higher growth rates, Greenspan counseled Clinton, the fastest route would be to cut the deficit, which in turn would reassure bond markets, lower the cost of credit, and increase productive investment. If Clinton cut the deficit, Greenspan would help by giving the program the Fed's seal of approval. Though Greenspan professed no influence over long-term rates, the bond market in fact closely takes its cue from the Fed's behavior on short-term rates, which signals the Fed's own expectations on inflation.

Clinton, famously, was outraged that his presidency was being held hostage by "a bunch of fucking bond traders." But he went with the program, a strategy directly opposed to the logic of Keynesian economics. In the economics of the Clinton-Greenspan grand bargain, you increased prosperity not by taxing or borrowing to provide concrete benefits and stimulating the purchasing power of ordinary people. Rather, you increased prosperity almost entirely via private financial market mechanisms—lower deficits leading to lower interest rates, which in turn would lower capital costs for businesses and consumer credit. But that approach meant that the more progressive parts of Clinton's program were boxed in—less money for public investment, education, and training, and less room for a middle-class tax cut. The Greenspan formula made Clinton even more of a centrist president. As the dissenter among Clinton's advisers, Joseph Stiglitz, chair of the Council of Economic Advisers and Nobel laureate, later wrote in his book *The Roaring Nineties*, "we pushed deficit reduction too far." The economy would have done better, Stiglitz argued, had the money been invested in "R&D, technology, infrastructure and education," rather than just cutting the deficit.

But here's the oddest part of the story. Clinton delivered on his part of the deal. The deficit was cut from 3.7 percent of GDP in 1993 to 2.1 percent in 1995, to just 0.3 percent in 1997. Contrary to Greenspan's economics lesson, the bond market did not reciprocate. After Clinton's budget deal in 1993 to cut the deficit by $140 billion by 1997, the interest rate on thirty-year mortgages and Treasury bonds actually went up, then went down, then went back up. In May 1997, the thirty-year Treasury bond, at just under 7 percent, was precisely what it had been in May 1993 when deficits were far higher. Nor did Greenspan even deliver on the part of monetary policy that he controlled. For Clinton's first four years, the Fed kept short-term rates high as well, because Greenspan himself continued to be overly worried about inflation. So Greenspan's economics were all wrong—both the theory and the execution.

Clinton, however, did get his recovery—but for reasons having nothing to do with deficit reduction. In Clinton's first term, improved growth and job creation reflected the benefits of new digital technologies, falling inflation rates, a decline in oil prices, and a recovery from the recession of 1990–91. Bond markets basically ignored his politically costly deficit reduction. In his second term, the recovery became an unsustainable bubble—driven by financial market speculation and borrowing, all supercharged by deregulation and by Federal Reserve monetary policy that helped inflate the bubble rather than contain it.

Why did the Fed not pursue its usual policy of "taking away the punch bowl" when the economy was roaring? Greenspan mistakenly focused on product prices, which were stable, and not on soaring financial asset prices like stocks and real estate, which he felt were best left to markets. In addition, the Clinton administration's pressure on developing countries to open their financial markets to speculative capital inflows led to a series of financial crises in Mexico, Russia, and much of East Asia. That in turn led the Federal Reserve to flood global financial markets with cheap dollars.

At home, cheaper money, deregulation, and a rising stock market made borrowing all the more attractive. Households also increased their debt, partly to compensate for stagnant wages. Earlier generations had paid off mortgages. This generation borrowed against their housing wealth. The net savings rate (savings minus borrowing) fell from 9.4 percent in the 1970s and 9.0 percent in the 1980s to just 3.3 percent in Clinton's final four years in office. The British political economist Colin Crouch gave this trend a name—"privatized Keynesianism." With real Keynesianism, government borrowed and spent when the economy was soft. The policy was constructively "counter-cyclical"—government leaning against the wind. But private Keynesianism was *pro-cyclical*. Households and financiers borrowed when times were good, creating bubbles; and then when the crash came and the economy needed stimulus, they couldn't borrow. The "wealth effects" of the stock market bubble, according to a study by two Fed economists, Dean Maki and Michael Palumbo, increased consumer spending by three to five cents for every additional dollar of paper financial wealth. Economist Dean Baker calculated that the stock market bubble added $5 trillion to paper net worth, most of it concentrated at the top, which translated to $150 billion to $200 billion in additional annual spending.

The Clinton boom, in short, had little to do with Clinton's economic policies other than financial deregulation—which helped inflate an unsustainable bubble. Ordinarily given to Delphic pronouncements, Greenspan candidly expressed his worry in a famous 1996 speech warning about "irrational exuberance." Greenspan knew that bubbles are notoriously hard to deflate gently. They tend to expand until they pop. But he missed the source of the bubble: the greater the financial deregulation, the more the opportunities for debt-financed speculation, just as in the 1920s. The best way to prevent the cycle of bubble and crash is to have well-regulated financial markets, something out of fashion in the 1990s.

Greenspan hoped he could talk the inflated market down, even as he eased interest rates. That failed. The tech-heavy NASDAQ rose from 800 in 1994 to over 5,000 in March 2000, before crashing more than 80 percent when the dot-com and telecom stock bubble burst. This crash was contained, but it was a harbinger of the far more pervasive and damaging collapse of 2008.

At the time, Clinton and the New Democrats claimed credit for a decade of growth and job creation. But the prosperity was illusory and the policies perverse. Clinton's legacy was a set of shibboleths that created bubble prosperity during Clinton's second term, but were toxic for Democrats and ordinary working families over the long term—budget balance, financial deregulation, globalism as defined by and for finance, and limited use of the public sector—the opposite of Roosevelt's New Deal. Tragically, these policies would be echoed by those of Barack Obama, despite far more auspicious circumstances for a New Deal revival.

7

Obama's Missed Moment

On September 15, 2008, the financial system collapsed. The crash began with the insolvency of the venerable investment banking firm Lehman Brothers. Lehman had been underwriting and trading highly speculative securities, using money borrowed in short-term financial markets, with only a thin cushion of its own capital. When the bets went bad, nobody wanted to lend the firm more money, and Lehman was suddenly broke.

The practice was not unique to Lehman. In a deregulated financial system, extensive borrowing and speculation on thin capital had become a pervasive profit strategy for the largest banks. Trading had displaced traditional underwriting. Deregulation had placed these reckless strategies beyond the purview of the regulators.

As investors fled, debts went unpaid, other major banks scrambled to raise cash; and overnight the collapse spread to the largest financial houses in the system. Even banks that did not pursue strategies like Lehman's were creditors of those that did. In a forced marriage the very next day, the Federal Reserve bankrolled the $50 billion acquisition of Merrill Lynch by Bank of America. The government also took over the American International Group, which had gone bust underwriting derivatives. The collapse of several other financial firms followed. This would not have been possible in the well-regulated financial economy created by the New Deal, but those regulations had long since been scrapped.

Warren Buffett once observed, "You never know who is swimming naked until the tide goes out." The receding tide revealed that the entire, interconnected financial system had been making thinly capitalized, naked bets. By week's end, debts exceeded capital by a large margin and sufficient money was simply not available, even under the Fed's emergency authority to flood the system with cash. Treasury Secretary Hank Paulson later testified that all but one of the largest money-center banks were insolvent. Had government not stepped in, the general economic collapse would have been worse than in 1929, since credit was effectively frozen. This was not a crisis of liquidity—temporary shortages of funds—something the Fed could handle. It was a deeper crisis of solvency.

On September 18, three days into the collapse, Fed Chair Ben Bernanke and Treasury Secretary Hank Paulson met with senior congressional leaders of both parties and explained that the entire credit system had seized up. The entire economy could follow. This was worse than 1929. They begged—Paulson literally got down on his knees—for an emergency infusion of $700 billion for Treasury to buy securities that suddenly had no market value, in order to replenish the capital of key financial institutions. These were mostly bonds and derivatives backed by subprime mortgages, a complex and lucrative scam enabled by the deregulation promoted by both parties.

The timing of the collapse, less than two months before the election, was providential for Barack Obama and the Democrats. The crash occurred on the watch of George W. Bush, and it was the result of the conservative ideology of letting markets run riot. Given that the emergency relief program required the active collaboration of both parties, Barack Obama as the Democratic nominee was quickly drawn into the negotiations of how to proceed. Both in the private sessions and in televised ones, Obama performed more impressively than either Bush or the Republican nominee, John McCain.

On September 25, Bush invited congressional leaders of both parties and the two presidential candidates to an emergency meeting at the White House. He began by warning the group that if Congress didn't act fast, "this sucker's going to go down."

A version of the bank recapitalization bill, called the Troubled Asset Relief Program (TARP), was enacted by Congress on October 3. Most House Democrats voted for it, and most Republicans voted against. Democrats attached two conditions: $75 billion was set aside for relief of homeowners at risk of foreclosure, and there would be a Congressional Oversight Panel with subpoena power to monitor how the Treasury and the Fed were spending the money. Harry Reid, the Senate majority leader, appointed as chair of the panel a Harvard bankruptcy law expert named Elizabeth Warren.

As the Obama administration and the Fed mainly did the bidding of the biggest banks, Warren and the oversight panel would become one of two sources of loyal opposition calling for a far more radical, Rooseveltian approach. The other was the FDIC, which was the last regulatory hawk in laissez-faire Washington, because its own trust funds had to be tapped to pay depositors when an insured bank failed. The chair of the FDIC was a tough and savvy regulator named Sheila Bair. She was, of all things, a Republican, having been appointed by George W. Bush—and sat well to the left of Obama's incoming economic team.

The financial collapse should have set up Obama to orchestrate a resurrection of the New Deal—the containment of the toxic tendencies of private finance, the expansion of government to do what markets could not, and the use of the crisis as an object lesson. Yet Obama's administration was an opportunity lost and a crisis wasted. Most of what he did propped up the banking system rather than cleaning it out or seriously re-regulating finance. Economic inequality continued to widen. Obama's obsession with deficit reduction made the recovery far too slow. Bush's collapse became Obama's recession, producing Democratic losses in the 2010 midterm of sixty-three seats, exceeding even the Clinton losses of 1994. That in turn reverberated with massive Democratic losses at the state level, giving Republicans vital control of redistricting after the 2010 Census.

Like Clinton, Obama managed to win his own reelection. Both had luck on their side. Neither of the losing Republican candidates in 1996 and 2012, Robert Dole and Mitt Romney, had a populist bone in their bodies. So the pent-up popular frustration against the failure of both parties to address the upward tilt of the economy would continue to fester, until the faux-populist political explosion of 2016.

Until June 2008, candidate Obama had only the most rudimentary team of economic advisers. He had come to prominence as a youthful idealist and a critic of Bush's foreign policy, especially the Iraq War. He also thrilled Democratic voters as potentially the first African American president. Obama did not expect that he would be presiding over a severe economic crisis. Early in his campaign, his top two economic staffers were a moderately liberal economist of no national reputation, Austan Goolsbee, Obama's colleague from the University of Chicago; and a progressive law professor and respected critic of financial excess, Daniel Tarullo, who in the 1990s had worked in the Clinton White House and then as assistant secretary of state for economic affairs. Tarullo, studying the impact of global deregulation on bank solvency in the early 2000s, had become somewhat radicalized on the issue of financial regulation. These advisers were occasionally joined by Paul Volcker, who had been impressed with Obama, and volunteered his services early on. Robert Rubin, as a good trader covering his bets, was simultaneously offering advice during the primaries to both Hillary Clinton and Obama. Rubin's son Jamie was working as a major fundraiser for Obama.

During primary season, Obama's one major speech on the impending economic crisis, at Cooper Union on March 27, was stunningly progressive. Coming just days after the collapse of Bear Stearns, which prefigured the general financial collapse in September, Obama's speech called for a complete overhaul of the financial system. He declared: "Under Republican and Democratic administrations, we've failed to guard against practices that too often rewarded financial manipulation instead of productivity and sound business practice. We let the special interests put their thumbs on the economic scales. The result has been a distorted market that creates bubbles instead of sustained economic growth; a market that favors Wall Street over Main Street, and ends up hurting both."

The speech was a pointed critique not just of Bush but of the Clintons. And it went well beyond generalizations to provide a detailed reform blueprint. The impending crisis, Obama explained, had been seeded by the manipulations of financial engineers who had created categories of products that defied existing regulatory categories, and the willful failure of captured or corrupted regulators to keep up with deceptive market innovations. But, said Obama, no amount of evasion or manipulation should be tolerated. "We need to regulate institutions for what they do, not for what they are." Specifically, he added, "Capital requirements should be strengthened, particularly for complex financial instruments like some of the mortgage securities that led to our current crisis." And Obama's diagnosis of the regulatory failure singled out the political power of capital. "This was not the invisible hand at work. Instead, it was the hand of industry lobbyists tilting the playing field in Washington."

The speech had been drafted by Tarullo and carefully reviewed and revised by Obama. Coming six months before the deeper September collapse, it was both radical and prophetic. But it was the last such speech Obama would give during two terms as president. When Obama as president actually had the power to make such changes, he opted instead to prop up the existing system. Today, the largest money-center banks are larger, more profitable, and more concentrated than ever. Systemic risks persist.

Less than three months after the Cooper Union speech, when it was clear that he would be the nominee, Obama downgraded Goolsbee and Tarullo, marginalized Volcker, and brought in a Wall Street–friendly economic team. In this maneuver, there was another invisible hand at work—that of Robert Rubin. As the prospect of a major financial crisis worsened, Obama's more conservative advisers and large donors persuaded him that he needed to bring in the A-team, people with senior experience in the financial industry and in government. These turned out to be mostly alums of the Clinton administration or other allies of Rubin.

As coordinator of his economic team, Obama brought in a young Rubin protégé named Jason Furman, whose main qualification was that he directed a program housed at Brookings and funded by Rubin called the Hamilton Project. (Furman had also studied with Stiglitz, but in 2008 his politics were more those of Rubin.) The Hamilton Project sponsored small-bore policy initiatives to create economic opportunity around the edges of a structurally unequal economy without fundamentally tampering with the core privileged role of Wall Street or the gospels of deregulation, free trade, and budget balance. With Furman now as quarterback closely consulting with Rubin, the door was opened to bringing back a far more orthodox and finance-friendly economic team.

By fall, Volcker had been dispatched to head an advisory council with no influence. The power players were Rubin's former deputy, Larry Summers, as head of the National Economic Council; and another Rubin protégé, Tim Geithner, as treasury secretary. In Geithner's previous post as president of the New York Federal Reserve Bank, he had been selected by a panel headed by an ultra deficit hawk, investment banker Peter G. Peterson. Other key economic officials named by Obama were Mike Froman as the top trade official with seats on both the National Economic Council and National Security Council, and Peter Orszag as head of Office of Management and Budget. Orszag had worked as an economic adviser to Clinton and was personally close to Rubin. After Orszag's tenure with Obama, Rubin got him a lucrative post at Citigroup as a managing director and vice chair of investment banking. Froman had been Rubin's chief of staff at the Clinton Treasury. He followed Rubin to a Citigroup job as head of emerging markets. Froman worked in Obama's 2004 Senate campaign and it was Froman who introduced Obama to Rubin.

The two more progressive outliers on the economic team were Christy Romer, an academic economist from Berkeley, and Jared Bernstein, who had come from the Economic Policy Institute. Romer and Bernstein were regularly overruled by Summers, Geithner, and Chief of Staff Rahm Emanuel. Bernstein's title, interestingly, was economic adviser to Vice President Joe Biden.

Thus, despite the worst financial collapse since 1929, which should have called into question all elements of the economic orthodoxy, allies of Wall Street were safely ensconced in all the key Obama power positions. There would be no fundamental change in the Wall Street money machine or the conflicts of interest on which it was built. Indeed, several of the top officials epitomized those conflicts, using their time in government to make policies friendly to Wall Street and then leaving government to take Wall Street jobs paying annual salaries well into the millions.

Robert Rubin is the emblematic figure in this story of the capture of successive Democratic presidents and candidates by the financial industry. In 1992, when Clinton turned to Rubin to head his economic team, Rubin was co-chair of America's top investment bank, Goldman Sachs. After serving as treasury secretary for part of Clinton's second term, Rubin in 1999 left government to chair the executive committee of Citigroup, then the nation's top commercial bank. While in government, Rubin worked hard to kill the last vestiges of the Glass-Steagall Act, which he finally accomplished with its formal repeal in 1999. Rubin was a close ally of Sanford Weill, the financier who gradually assembled the empire of insurance, commercial banking, and investment-banking pieces that ultimately became Citigroup. When Congress formally repealed Glass-Steagall in November 1999 with the Gramm-Leach-Bliley Act, the legislation was termed in some circles the "Citigroup Authorization Act." Rubin stepped down as treasury secretary just before Clinton signed the repeal. Four months later, Weill welcomed Rubin as the new chairman of Citi's executive committee, with total annual compensation that soon reached around $40 million.

Under Clinton, Rubin was a key player in getting Congress to pass legislation making it illegal for any branch of government to regulate financial derivatives, artificial securities that are one or two or even three levels removed from underlying assets. In a famous episode in May 1998, Brooksley Born, then the chair of the Commodity Futures Trading Commission, had sent out a "concept release" soliciting comments on the need to regulate over-the-counter derivatives (those not traded on exchanges), which had become a highly lucrative, highly leveraged, and largely opaque realm of finance. Born was concerned, prophetically, that a crash of derivatives could crash the economy. In a notorious call recounted by Born's chief of staff Michael Greenberger, Larry Summers, Rubin's protégé and successor as treasury secretary, phoned Born and warned, "I have thirteen bankers in my office, and they say if you go forward with this you will cause the worst financial crisis since World War II."

What actually caused the worst financial crisis since World War II, of course, was the *failure* to regulate credit derivatives and kindred toxic products laden with conflicts of interest, lack of transparency, and above all excess leverage. Born soon resigned. Just to make sure no level of government would ever regulate over-the-counter credit derivatives, Rubin and his allies fashioned legislation called the Commodity Futures Modernization Act of 2000. It prohibited the federal government from regulating credit derivatives either as securities or as insurance. In an unintended burst of candor given what derivatives really are, the new law also prohibited state governments from regulating derivatives as gambling.

Rubin is worth more than passing notice in our larger story of the Democrats' defection from the New Deal, not out of some conspiratorial sense that he personally called all the shots, but as the emblem of an era. In the old days, Rubin would have been called a power broker, an influence-peddler, or a fixer. But those labels didn't attach, because Rubin's manner seemed so public-minded, so socially liberal, and so self-effacingly nice. Rubin's rise, however, was not just personal but structural. It reflected, and reinforced, the pervasive influence of finance on the American economy and polity, through both deregulated financial markets and campaign money. His extraordinary power reflected the synergy and networking of his multiple roles—as fundraiser, gatekeeper, banker, certifier of fiscal soundness, and as the man reputedly responsible for the boom of the 1990s.

Rubin's reach into the overlapping worlds of corporate and Wall Street boardrooms, nonprofits, party organs, and senior Democratic politicians was without parallel. It was Rubin who maneuvered Larry Summers into the presidency of Harvard, certified Summers's supposed new maturity, and resisted Summers's ouster. Rubin was one of only seven members of the Harvard Corporation, yet characteristically, when the Summers presidency exploded, little mud splattered on Rubin.

As Clinton's top economic adviser, Rubin provided other dubious advice that included making NAFTA a top priority, letting China into the WTO with no enforceable commitments for serious reforms, pushing the budget all the way to surplus, and devising a bipartisan process to put deficit reduction on an automatic formula that could include cuts in Social Security. These views are not just those of a centrist policy kibitzer. They are exactly what you would expect of a leading banker.

Rubin's multiple roles made him a walking conflict of interest, as in the case of the Glass-Steagall repeal. Rubin's old firm, Goldman Sachs, just happened to be the single biggest underwriter of Mexican bonds both before and immediately after the passage of NAFTA, as well as the investment bank that arranged the privatization of the Mexican national phone company. After NAFTA created a gold rush of foreign money into Mexico (enriching Goldman and its clients) and triggered an unsustainable speculative boom followed by a bust, Rubin conceived and lobbied for the bailout of Mexico to make foreign bondholders whole. A little noticed provision of NAFTA permitted foreign banks to acquire Mexican ones. In 2001, Rubin, back in the private sector, negotiated the $12.5 billion purchase of Mexico's leading bank, Banamex, for Citigroup.

In his role as Clinton's adviser in trade negotiations, Rubin's top priority was not a level playing field for American exports but access for U.S. financial capital. When China was seeking WTO membership in 1999, Rubin blocked the deal until Beijing satisfied Rubin's conditions on access for foreign banks. Other concerns were dropped.

In November 2001, as the infamous energy company Enron

was collapsing, Rubin phoned Peter Fisher, undersecretary of the Treasury for domestic finance, to suggest that Treasury might intervene with credit-rating agencies to delay a downgrading of Enron's debt. Enron owed Citi about $750 million. Fisher wisely fended off the pressure. When word leaked out of Rubin's lobbying, the Treasury and "a close associate of Rubin" issued nicely complementary statements, so that Rubin's inquiry was played by the press as tentative, hypothetical, and above all public-minded.

Rubin was treated almost as a cult figure. In 1999, along with Summers and Greenspan, he was the subject of an adoring *Time* magazine cover story headlined "The Committee to Save the World." But if the world's financial markets needed saving, it was because the policies of Rubin and company demanded that they open to speculative finance—and they now needed to be bailed out by the U.S. Treasury and the Fed.

When the Democrats were out of power, between 2000 and 2008, Rubin's influence as the Democrats' economic seer continued. In April 2004, AFL-CIO president John Sweeney proposed a private meeting with Democratic nominee John Kerry to discuss living standards as a campaign issue, and the candidate invited the labor leader to his Beacon Hill home. Sweeney arrived at the Kerry manse, bringing his policy director, Chris Owens, and Jeff Faux of the Economic Policy Institute. There, seated in the elegant living room, were Robert Rubin and two longtime lieutenants, investment banker and former Rubin deputy Roger Altman, and fellow Clinton alum Gene Sperling—Kerry's key economic advisers.

In a three-hour conversation, the group discussed the deficit, taxes, trade, health care, unions, and living standards. At length, Kerry announced that the meeting needed to wrap up, because "Bob has to get back to Washington." Rubin responded that, no, he could stay as long as Kerry wanted. Sweeney and colleagues were ushered out the door. Rubin, Altman, and Sperling remained. "Wall Street was in the room before we arrived," Jeff Faux commented to me, "and they were there after we left."

When the Democrats took back the House in 2006, incoming Speaker Nancy Pelosi scheduled two briefings for the new Democratic Caucus. One, on defense, included three experts of differing views. The other, on the economy, featured Robert Rubin appearing solo. When Obama became president, Rubin had easy access to any of several top economic and regulatory appointees, who were all protégés or personal beneficiaries of jobs he'd gotten them in the years between Clinton and Obama. The era of Rubin's outsized influence began with Walter Mondale in 1984 and only ended fully thirty-six years later in 2020 when Joe Biden, at last, hired none of Rubin's allies.

The serial forms of deregulation that finally crashed the economy in September 2008 had been building and cumulating for several decades. Three earlier crashes, harbingers of the general collapse of 2008, had been contained because the degree of leverage, opacity, conflicts of interest, deregulation, non-supervision, and above all interpenetration had not quite reached the level of the early 2000s. But each was a clear warning that went unheeded.

The first of these was the savings and loan collapse of the 1990s. Thanks to a bipartisan legislative deal sponsored by two legislators who were allies of financial speculators, Republican Jake Garn of Utah and Democrat Freddie St. Germain of Rhode Island, savings and loans, which had been sleepy, well-regulated local lenders with modest profits and rare scandals, were freed by the Garn-St. Germain Act of 1982 to become far more speculative. S&Ls were now allowed to venture far afield from housing finance and make commercial loans and even invest in junk bonds. On the deposit side, tiny S&Ls could offer higher interest rates than the going rate, and become national powerhouse institutions overnight, with very thin capital. Faced with these temptations, S&Ls engaged in massive speculations, often corruptly. Between 1986 and 1995, 1,043 of the nation's 3,234 savings and loan associations failed. More than a thousand executives were convicted in criminal prosecutions for fraud, kickbacks, and self-dealing, and several went to prison. In the end, Congress had to bail out the industry to the tune of $124 billion. It was the largest cascade of bank failures since the early 1930s. But unlike the larger collapse of 2008, the S&L industry was less interconnected with the larger banking system, so the crisis could be contained.

A second collapse that should have been a warning was the crash of Long-Term Capital Management. LTCM was a hedge fund based in Greenwich, Connecticut, whose advisers included two Nobel laureates. Its investment strategy was based on making highly technical bets on anomalies of financial markets—in the form of two almost identical securities trading at slightly different prices—which its model predicted would inevitably converge, allowing the hedge fund to make big profits using borrowed money. To finance its activities, LTCM relied heavily on credit derivatives, which allowed it to make massive bets with very little of its own capital. At the beginning of 1998, LTCM had equity of $4.7 billion, and debts totaling $124.5 billion, a ratio of 25 to 1. In addition, the hedge fund had derivative exposure in excess of a trillion dollars.

When financial crises occurred in East Asia and Russia in 1997–98, they caused various stocks and bonds to move in unexpected directions that defied LTCM's financial modeling. The hedge fund rapidly burned through its equity and could not pay its massive debts. The debts were disguised through the use of derivatives. Thanks to the loophole in the Investment Company Act under which hedge funds operated, no government entity had an overview of LTCM's books, trading strategy, or exposure.

When LTCM and its creditors asked the New York Federal

Reserve Bank for urgent help, Fed officials looking at the numbers realized that LTCM's debt to so many institutions was so large that an abrupt collapse could literally wipe out the equity of many banks and thus crash the financial system. It was an exact preview of what did occur in 2008. On September 23, 1998, the New York Fed summoned the heads of New York's major commercial and investment banks to an emergency meeting, where it requested them to "voluntarily" come up with over $3.6 billion so that LTCM's losses could be liquidated over time without crashing the system. The largest banks ponied up $300 million each. They could afford it. In a case of poetic justice, the one large investment bank that refused to participate was Bear Stearns, whose own collapse in March 2008 was the first of several.

But note—LTCM was just one firm, and it took "only" $3.6 billion to keep its collapse contained. Surely, if the actions of a single firm nearly crashed the whole economy, regulators should have paid attention to the entire pattern. But they did not. By 2008, when tactics like those used by LTCM were pervasive, there was not enough money in the system for the Fed to organize a voluntary private bailout; and it took fully $700 billion in government funds to begin to recapitalize the banks and contain the wider collapse.

Astonishingly, the LTCM affair led to no wider reforms. Too many people were making too much money. No additional regulations were applied to hedge funds. When I interviewed Robert Rubin in 2007 and asked him if he thought there was a case for greater regulation of hedge funds, he seemed puzzled by the question. The system's extreme leverage and opacity only increased. When Lehman collapsed in 2008 its leverage ratio was at least double that of LTCM. And the leverage of AIG was effectively infinite: it was writing derivatives contracts, de facto insurance policies to pay investors if securities defaulted, with no loss reserves whatever.

One more episode should have been a warning shot to the system—the dot-com and telecom stock market crash of 2000. Once again, this was the result of the interplay of deregulation and corruption. After telecommunications were deregulated in 1996, there was a gold rush to create new telecom companies, either through mergers or from scratch. The result was temporarily inflated stock prices, disguising massive excess capacity.

One aspect of the fraud that followed was conflicts of interest on the part of stock analysts. Supposedly independent specialists who were there to serve investors in fact cynically touted high-risk telecom stocks that their investment banker colleagues were underwriting. The analysts were well aware that many of the stocks were all but worthless, and their colleagues were dumping these stocks as fast as the public could be induced to buy them. Here again, most were punished by slaps on the wrist.

Another aspect of the crash was fraudulent accounting. The emblematic case was the Enron collapse. Deregulation of electricity allowed Enron to operate as both an energy supplier and an energy trader. Enron borrowed heavily to finance its speculations, and artificially inflated the value of its own stock. Executives disguised the extent of its debt by creating "special purpose vehicles" to hold debt that was not shown on Enron's balance sheet, even though Enron was ultimately responsible for the debt. Enron's accounting and audit firm, Arthur Andersen, colluded in the deception. All of this was the opposite of the transparent and efficient energy competition that sponsors of deregulation had promised.

Here again, there was an echo of one aspect of the fraud and excess of the 1920s—hyped stocks, faked books, and conflicted stock touts. But in the dot-com and Enron collapses, as in the S&L crisis, there was not enough contagion with the banks to crash the system. When the stock market crashed in 2000, a lot of investors lost a lot of money, but the larger economy went on. And so did the larger system of deregulated financial markets. Investment bankers had underwritten stocks of firms that faked books and went broke, but the investment banks had limited their own exposure by unloading the stocks on unwary investors—another echo of the 1920s.

It was mainly the accounting profession that took the fall. Until the 1980s, the big eight accounting firms, like the S&Ls, had been fairly staid and clean operations. Nobody got filthy rich being an accountant. The securities laws required companies to get annual audits, and the audits were entrusted to firms governed by their own codes of ethics. In the go-go 1980s, the big accounting firms like Arthur Andersen realized they could make a lot more money selling consulting services. A company like Enron or WorldCom, inclined to fiddle its books to deceive investors, could hire an accounting firm to advise it on how to rig its accounts and still pass the audit—which was conveniently conducted by the same accounting firm.

A noble if boring industry was soon disgraced by gross conflicts of interest. When Enron went down, Arthur Andersen went down with it. This colossal systemic failure resulted in only one modest reform, the Sarbanes-Oxley Act of 2002, which tightened audit requirements and created a new entity under the SEC to supervise the accounting profession.

Sarbanes-Oxley made everyone feel better—here was reform legislation at last. But the accountants were bit players in the deeper corruption. Making the accountants scapegoats was on a par with going after the piano player in the brothel. The larger pattern of speculative abuse that finally crashed the entire system in 2008 was left untouched.

Supposedly, deregulation made financial markets more efficient. But whatever small efficiencies might have been gained were swamped by the systemic costs of the eventual 2008 collapse. The economy lost at least $15 trillion in GDP. Homeowners lost $7 trillion in equity. Millions of workers lost their jobs. De-regulation also supercharged the economy's gross inequality by creating a new class of billionaires, all of whom were either from financial firms exempted from regulation or from digital monop-olies exempt from antitrust law. These extreme wealth concentra-tions overwhelmed the modest direct outlays of the Clinton and Obama administrations on behalf of greater equality.

One increasingly pernicious area of American capitalism fa-cilitated by serial bouts of deregulation is the growing sector of hedge funds and private equity. Private equity adds nothing to the real productive wealth of the economy. It is parasitic on actual businesses and their workers. The whole system is rooted in the abuse of four provisions of law—the original exemption for private investment companies in the 1940 Investment Company Act, which was widened over time; the right to take a tax deduc-tion for borrowed money; the abuse of the bankruptcy code; and the absence of any rules regarding conflicts of interest between owners and the companies they acquire. The loopholes that were added to the securities laws, allowing much larger numbers of investors to put money into private equity, were mainly the work of Democrats. The key law was an obscure special interest bill with the Orwellian name the National Securities Markets Im-provement Act of 1996. It was the handiwork of Bill Clinton and Robert Rubin.

The typical private equity strategy is to look for a company with substantial cash reserves or real estate assets, buy the com-pany almost entirely with borrowed money, and put the debt on the balance sheet of the acquired company. The company is then stuck with the expense of the interest on the debt, at high rates. The new private equity owners then pay themselves "special dividends," looting the operating company still further. Going forward, they charge management fees, pulling out more prof-its at the expense of the business. As costs exceed income due to the parasitic role of the private equity owners, the new owners look for ways to cut costs. Typically these tactics include cuts in worker wages and benefits, as well as layoffs. When they can get away with it, the private equity owners also cash out worker pension funds. And when the acquired company owns real estate, as many retailers do, the private equity owners typically sell the real estate, pocket the cash, and often arrange a leaseback deal, sticking the operating company with new rental costs. When Bain Capital took over KB Toys in 2000, it put up just 6 percent and borrowed the rest. Before KB went bankrupt, costing ten thousand jobs, Bain realized a gain of 360 percent on its original investment.

A bankruptcy is of no consequence to the private equity owner, who has often extracted several times their small cash investment long before the operating company collapses. On the contrary, bankruptcy creates new opportunities for private equity. In bankruptcy, the worker pension fund can be eliminated or drastically cut. Often, the same consortium of private equity owners that has driven the company into insolvency is able to buy it out of bankruptcy, persuade a bankruptcy judge to settle its debts at so many cents on the dollar, and begin the parasitic cycle anew.

Note that this entire scam is at odds with the usual disciplines attributed to efficient capitalism. We learn in Economics 101 that the definition of an entrepreneur is someone who takes a risk. If the enterprise thrives, the risk is rewarded. If the enterprise fails, the entrepreneur loses. With private equity, that premise is turned on its head. Private equity firms and creators of collateralized debt obligation (CDO) securities both fob off the risk on someone else. The parasitic private equity firm or investment banker makes money *even if the underlying enterprise fails.* Indeed, in the case of private equity, the entire business strategy of the private equity firm of piling on debt and extracting fees and assets increases the risk that the enterprise *will* fail.

Since 2009, investors have put some $5.8 trillion into private equity, a sum that has been heavily leveraged as private equity firms borrow money to acquire companies. Some estimates value the total private equity holdings at $11 trillion. Today, some 35,000 companies employing about 6 million workers are owned by private equity. The impact has been concentrated in some sectors, such as nursing homes, retail, and newspapers, where it has been devastating. One comprehensive study found that when a nursing home was acquired by a private equity firm, standards declined and fatalities increased. This is all too predictable, since the standard private equity strategy is to reduce pay and staffing levels. Since 2000, private equity investments in nursing homes have increased from about $5 billion to more than $100 billion.

In the case of regional newspapers, large private equity companies have purchased thousands of dailies and weeklies. Their model of stripping assets to maximize their own profits has deprived American communities of the news coverage that is essential to informed civic life. Newsrooms are often cut by 50 to 80 percent after private equity takeovers, creating what critics have termed "news deserts." This is especially pronounced in state capitals where the wreckage of local newspapers has impoverished coverage of governors, legislatures, and corruption. More than 1,400 cities and towns lost their newspaper in the fifteen years between 2004 and 2019. The prevailing assumption is that newspapers have been undermined mainly as the internet has become a dominant source of news, and their most reliable traditional source of revenue, classified ads, have been crowded out by web-based services such as Craigslist. In fact, several studies have shown that independently owned newspapers, though not as lucrative as in the glory years before the internet, are able to turn a small profit. It's not the internet that's killing them; it's private equity.

Retail is a similar story. Street-level shops are a vital part of the life of communities. Empty storefronts and half-vacant malls are a sign of local economic ill-health. This is a part of the market economy that complements the civic part. Plentiful competition in retail makes that sector of capitalism function according to the laws of supply and demand. To some extent, Amazon and other sources of direct online sales are cutting into the market share of local retail and traditional national chains. But here again, a major culprit is private equity. Look at a press account of almost any bankruptcy of a large retailer, read down several paragraphs into the story, and you will invariably find that the owner is a private equity firm.

Private equity is another source of today's extreme concentrations of wealth. The essence of the model is that billions flow to owners, while worker pay, benefits, and job security are cut.

Rather than serving the real economy, as in the textbook story of capital markets supplying funds to consumers and businesses, the financial economy had become an engine of its own wealth. The banking industry's share of total profits in the economy went from less than 16 percent as late as 1986 to over 41 percent on the eve of the collapse. This was less a contribution to the real economy than a tax on it.

Whole libraries have been written on the specific abuses that led to the 2008 crash, and I've contributed two books of my own. To summarize a complex story, on a policy level the culprit was one part deliberate deregulation, and one part a studied incuriosity on the part of regulators as the financial industry came up with one "innovation" after another that was fraudulent and risky to the entire system. In the free-market climate of the entire era, financial innovations were deemed good by definition.

Laws already on the books gave regulators plenty of authority to crack down on abusive practices, but as the Brooksley Born affair demonstrated, the rare regulators who attempted to use their authority were overruled and ostracized. In other cases, regulators such as Alan Greenspan flatly refused to use the power they had. A law passed by the Democratic Congress in the aftermath of the savings and loan collapse, the Home Ownership and Equity Protection Act of 1994, gave the Federal Reserve the authority to crack down on the origination of unsound, high-risk variable rate mortgages known in the trade as "liar loans." But Greenspan believed that markets should be free to innovate, so he refused to act.

In this deregulated environment of intensified financial engineering, the two core abuses involved conflicts of interest between insiders and everyone else, and grossly excessive disguised leverage. The entire New Deal regulatory schema was intended to keep markets tolerably honest using a mix of disclosures and outright prohibitions. But those safeguards had long since been overtaken by either deregulation, non-regulation, "innovation," or outright fraud. When investigators shifted through the ashes of the collapse, one of the pervasive abuses they found was investment banking houses literally betting against their customers—peddling dubious securities with one hand and short-selling with the other.

A vivid example of how this all worked was the subprime scandal and resulting mortgage collapse. Subprime was at the heart of the larger collapse because of the pyramid of derivatives backed by mortgages. As the mortgage market was deregulated, Wall Street started creating more risky and exotic versions of one of FDR's inventions—securities backed by mortgages. The original version was sponsored in the 1930s by Fannie Mae. Fannie would borrow money from the Treasury and buy loans from banks and thrift institutions; the money would replenish the capacity of lenders to make more retail mortgage loans, and the payment of interest and principal on the loans would pay off the debt to the Treasury. Fannie was careful to insist on well-vetted loans, and the system worked like a Swiss watch. Nobody got rich, nobody went broke, and homeowners got reliable mortgages—until Wall Street started messing with the idea.

In the late 1970s, the investment banking firm of Salomon Brothers created private mortgage-backed securities. Soon Wall Street came up with the further idea of sorting mortgages into categories of supposed risk to the investor. Bonds backed by prime mortgages would pay a lower rate of return; riskier mortgages a higher rate. In 1984, the financial industry persuaded Congress to enact the Secondary Mortgage Market Enhancement Act, allowing investment bankers to set their own standards on mortgage loan quality and sell mortgage-backed bonds with no government standards or guarantee. This new deregulation was sold as increasing competition and liquidity, though in practice it mainly enriched middlemen. The actual rate on retail mortgages continued to closely track the thirty-year Treasury bond.

Mortgage-backed securities, now repackaged into bonds known as collateralized debt obligations, became more and more complex and opaque. They were rated by another private sector industry whose entire business model was a conflict of interest, the so-called bond-rating agencies (actually for-profit firms). There were three big ones: Moody's, Standard & Poor, and Fitch. Taking an approach rather like that of the corrupted accounting firms, a bond-rating agency seeking repeat business would give the bond the triple-A rating that its packager wanted, without asking too many questions. Bond-rating agencies were, and remain, unregulated.

Meanwhile, Fannie Mae had been privatized and was concerned about maximizing its own profits. After staying away from bonds backed by sketchy mortgages and leaving that to Wall Street, Fannie began worrying about market share, and joined the subprime party in the years after 2001. Serving as one more corrupted enabler of the collapse, Fannie, once a clean New Deal public institution, would also have to be bailed out by the government.

Thus was the stage set for the collapse. In the 1990s, small segments of the mortgage industry had begun creating adjustable-rate mortgage products with very low "teaser" rates. These were not like ordinary variable-rate mortgages whose interest rate tracks a standard index reflecting the prime rate. Instead, they automatically "reset" to far higher rates after two or three years. They were appropriately nicknamed "exploding" loans. Further adding to the risk, loan applicants were encouraged to lie on the application about their income, assets, and work histories. In 2001, as the economy was suffering the effects of the dot-com crash, the Fed cut interest rates eleven times. With rock-bottom interest rates, housing values took off and subprime became a major business. The core mistake made by the Fed was to combine cheap money with lax regulation. It was an invitation to more speculation. As subprime took off after 2001, large mortgage banks such as Countrywide, Washington Mutual, Ameriquest, and HSBC Financial got into the subprime game.

Why would a lender make a mortgage loan to a borrower at high risk of defaulting? This perverse incentive was at the heart of the subprime fiasco. The reason was that the company originating the loan got rid of it as soon as the deal closed. The biggest Wall Street investment banks, including Goldman, Lehman, Bear Stearns, and JPMorgan Chase, made advance commitments to buy subprime loans that they could then package into collateralized debt obligation bonds, or CDOs. These in turn were unloaded to investors such as pension funds. By repackaging the debt into securities, the sponsors could disguise the fact that the underlying mortgage was likely to default. Thus neither the mortgage banker originating the subprime loan nor the investment bank packaging it held on to any risk.

Through a mysterious alchemy, the bond-rating process turned dross into gold. Bonds backed by packages of very risky mortgages somehow got triple-A ratings. The bond-rating companies did not even take a close look at the mortgages collateralizing the bonds. Insiders knew that at some point this house of cards had to collapse, but fortunes were being made in the meantime. A popular line on Wall Street was IBGYBG: I'll be gone, you'll be gone.

The pyramid scheme held up as long as interest rates were declining and housing prices were rising. Homebuyers who took out subprime mortgage loans were either deceived by mortgage companies and didn't appreciate the risks; or they gambled on rising housing prices and hoped that they could refinance their loan or sell their house at a profit before their adjustable rate exploded. Investigations later revealed that about half of the people talked into taking out subprime loans qualified for conventional fixed-rate mortgages. At both the retail level of mortgages and the wholesale levels of investment banks packaging mortgages into bonds, this was a Ponzi scheme.

By 2007, the house of cards was beginning to totter. As housing prices peaked and as homeowners faced sharply higher interest rates, mortgage defaults increased. As mortgages went bad, CDOs lost value. As CDOs lost value, investment bankers who had placed leveraged bets on them started suffering increasing losses. Likewise firms that wrote derivative contracts insuring the bonds. Banks that specialized in subprime suffered heavy losses as well. So interconnected was the financial system that it all crashed.

But it was ordinary people, not financial manipulators, who suffered. By the end of 2009, one home in four was now worth less than its mortgage debt. Eventually, about 10 million home-owners had their homes foreclosed.

As Obama's team took charge in January 2009, one key policy question was whether to replace the management of the large banks whose reckless and conflicted practices had led to the collapse—or just bail them out. For Elizabeth Warren and Sheila Bair, the answer was obvious. Put the largest banks through a bankruptcy process, let stockholders take the loss, put them into temporary government receivership, bring in new reform management, and eventually turn a clean and solvent bank back to the private sector. As Warren taught in her bankruptcy course at Harvard Law School, this was how a bankruptcy worked. It was also exactly the way the FDIC dealt with insolvent banks under its purview—take the bank into FDIC receivership, do an audit to tally its assets and liabilities, pay off the insured depositors, and either bring in new management, shut it down, or merge it with a larger and healthier bank. Bair later told an interviewer that both Citigroup and Merrill Lynch should have been put into a government receivership. She wrote in her memoirs that when she learned that Obama was naming Tim Geithner to be treasury secretary, "it was like a punch in the gut. I did not understand how someone who had campaigned on a 'change' agenda could appoint someone so involved in contributing to the financial mess that had gotten Obama elected. . . . The only explanation I could think of was that Bob Rubin had pushed him."

Warren and Bair lost this argument. The very idea of tossing out management at Bob Rubin's bank, Citigroup, was unthinkable, much less putting the bank into receivership. Rather, the team of Bernanke, Geithner, and Summers devised ways of pumping money into the banks and taking toxic securities off their books. The Fed created entire new categories of "facilities" with technically opaque names like the Term Asset Loan

Facility, whose purpose was to shovel money into the big banks. This strategy was dressed up in disarming and public-minded language about restoring confidence. But in the political economy of the bank bailouts, the purpose was to leave the system basically intact while giving the big banks more of a cushion.

The plan "worked." The biggest banks recovered from the collapse more powerful than ever. Despite the fact that the entire saga was rife with fraud and criminal conflicts of interest, the Obama Justice Department brought no criminal cases against the bank executives responsible, and settled for modest fines paid by the banks (effectively by their shareholders). The Dodd-Frank Act limited some of the worst abuses, but left the banks' basic business model intact and put the government even more squarely in the business of assuring the system's solvency without addressing the conflicts of interest. The version of the act drafted by the Obama administration was even weaker than the one that eventually passed Congress.

By mid-2009, the public found it hard to tell which political party was in the pocket of Wall Street and which one was defending the interests of ordinary people. This alliance between the Obama administration and the biggest banks helped enable the far right to construct a totally false narrative in which the subprime collapse and the deep recession that followed was the result of soft-minded liberals trying to extend homeownership to lower-income and minority people who could not afford it. This story was totally bogus. The subprime operators and their investment banker partners who crashed the economy had no interest whatever in expanding housing opportunities. They were just out to make money, in this case fraudulently.

There were in fact well-designed programs for expanding homeownership using conventional mortgages combined with financial counseling, and these had low default rates. Community lenders like ShoreBank of Chicago showed how it could be done—carefully review the creditworthiness of a loan applicant, provide a conventional fixed-rate loan, and provide counseling. In fact, the Community Reinvestment Act (CRA) of 1977, often cited by the right wing as the source of pressure on banks to make unwise loans, stated in so many words that banks should make credit available to communities "consistent with safe and sound" lending standards. Common sense dictated that these standards precluded liar loans and exploding mortgages. Had the Fed enforced CRA, there would have been no financial collapse.*

As the Obama administration bailed out the largest bankers, it did not help the community banks that had been responsible lenders, who were now the innocent victims of the collapse wrought on Wall Street. Citigroup, Goldman, and the others were deemed too big to fail. ShoreBank was too small to matter; it got no aid and was allowed to go under.

The failure of the administration to make clear which side it was on allowed the far right to become the bearer of popular grievances. In February 2009, a right-wing financial commentator, Rick Santelli, speaking from the floor of the Chicago Mercantile Exchange, made an extended rant live on CNBC, blaming liberals for the crash, treating the bailout as a rescue of improvident homeowners (rather than banks), and calling for a new Tea Party. "This is America," he yelled. "How many of you people want to pay for your neighbor's mortgage that has an extra bathroom and can't pay their bills?" This moment of fake populism, falsely putting bond traders and aggrieved citizens on the

---

* In an earlier life, working as a Senate investigator for Banking Committee chairman William Proxmire, I wrote the CRA. We deliberately put in the soundness language so that nobody could accuse the CRA of promoting risky loans.

same side, was the origin of the modern Tea Party movement—which became a ready-made constituency for Donald Trump.

The administration's misplaced loyalty to the big banks also worsened the mortgage disaster for homeowners. Democrats in Congress, aware of the deepening crisis of default and foreclosure, had deliberately added $75 billion for mortgage refinancing to the TARP program. But Obama's people, protective of bank balance sheets, made sure that the details of this program were left to the bankers. In the 1930s, FDR's equivalent of this relief program was called the Home Owners' Loan Corporation. It was easy to use, and eventually refinanced one mortgage in five so that people would not lose their homes to foreclosure. Obama's program, by contrast, allowed bankers to devise the rules for "loan modification" programs, which were not true refinancings, were hard to qualify for, and provided homeowners little relief. In the end, much of the $75 billion went unspent.

Obama, Summers, and Geithner fiercely opposed another reform that would have helped homeowners keep their homes and slow the collapse of housing values. The idea was that homeowners could use the bankruptcy process to discharge part of their mortgage debt, just as corporations do when they use bankruptcy to renegotiate debts and keep the business operating. This proposal, termed "cramdown" by an appalled financial industry, would have helped homeowners at the expense of bankers and holders of securitized debt. The industry had gotten Congress to pass a law in 1993 prohibiting homeowners from using the personal bankruptcy process to reduce their mortgage but keep their homes. Obama, given an opportunity to show which side he was on, sided with the bankers. Bank balance sheets took priority over household balance sheets. In April 2009, Sen. Dick Durbin sponsored an amendment permitting homeowners to use bankruptcy to keep their homes. With Obama opposed, the amendment narrowly lost, 45 to 51.

Obama and his economic team even opposed the modest step of prohibiting the big banks that had taken hundreds of billions in taxpayer bailout money from paying their executives large bonuses. The need for bank cooperation was cited in this anti-populist stance. So 2009, as the rest of the economy was still suffering, was a banner year for banker bonuses. Wall Street paid out a total of $120 billion to its executives and traders.

Obama, at an April 2, 2009, White House meeting with top bankers urging them not to oppose modest reforms, said, "My administration is the only thing standing between you and the pitchforks." But compare this with FDR's epic line about the bankers, when he accepted re-nomination in 1936: "They are unanimous in their hatred for me—and I welcome their hatred." Economically and politically, Obama belonged with the pitchforks. Instead, it was all too obvious that Obama stood with the bankers.

The comparison with FDR is appalling. Nobody could doubt which side Roosevelt was on.

One more massive yet avoidable economic and political error was Obama's view of budget deficits and public investment. The spending of the $787 billion 2009 Recovery Act (spread out over four years) proved too meager to promote a rapid and robust economic recovery. Once cuts in state spending were netted out, it added less than half a percentage point per year to public spending. Christy Romer, incoming chair of the Council of Economic Advisers, took a hard look at the numbers in December 2008. Romer calculated that the minimum stimulus needed to get unemployment on a downward path was $1.2 trillion. Summers and Emanuel directed her not to even mention that number to Obama. Romer later told an interviewer, "Geithner would say, 'Let's heal the banks. That would be good for the economy.' I would say, 'Let's heal the economy. That would be good for the banks.'"

In the fall of 2009, the unemployment rate was still 10 percent. Congressional leaders had pleaded with Obama to support a second stimulus package, but Obama had already been persuaded by his conservative economic advisers that the more urgent goal was deficit reduction; the recovery would presumably take care of itself. With no help from the White House, however, House Speaker Nancy Pelosi got the House to pass a second stimulus of $154 billion emphasizing jobs, by just four votes. Obama quietly arranged for it to die in the Senate.

In his 2010 State of the Union address, Obama gave top billing to deficit reduction. His advisers had persuaded him that the economy was well on the road to recovery, and the more important task was to reassure financial markets, Clinton-Rubin-Greenspan-style, by cutting the deficit. They decided to brand the summer of 2010 "Recovery Summer," a tactic that backfired when the economy turned out to be nowhere near recovery.

Obama's vehicle for getting the deficit down was a commission charged with putting the budget on automatic pilot, using formulas that would constrain spending if Congress failed to hit predetermined deficit reduction targets. The idea, long a favorite of Robert Rubin and Pete Peterson, was made flesh with the Bowles-Simpson Commission, headed by a conservative corporate Democrat, Erskine Bowles, and a retired Republican senator, Alan Simpson of Wyoming. When the legislation to create the commission failed to pass the Senate in January 2010, Obama created it by executive order.

The order required a supermajority of fourteen of the commission's eighteen members for its recommendations to take effect. The commission's report outlined a draconian plan to cut the deficit by $4 trillion. Given that there were a few progressives on the commission, the vote to approve the plan in December 2010 fell just short of the required supermajority. But as part of the 2012 budget deal, Obama accepted something very similar in the form of automatic "sequesters" that would kick in if Congress fail to reach specified deficit-reduction targets. These constrained public spending for the rest of the Obama presidency, and slowed the recovery from the 2008 collapse.

Thus Obama, in one key respect after another, both symbolically and in his policies, signaled that he was more on the side of bankers and fiscal conservatives than ordinary people whose lives had been upended by the collapse and deep recession that followed.

By combining this brand of economic conservatism with social liberalism that was a hard sell under the best of circumstances, Obama drove white working-class voters into the camp of Donald Trump. In fairness, Obama did much that was exemplary, in the area of foreign policy, climate, racial and gender justice, and in leading an administration largely free of scandal. But none of his great accomplishments was of much help to the pocketbook predicament of the common American.

Ever since Carter, Democrats had also joined Republicans as the party of tax cuts for the rich. The first supply-side tax cut was championed by Carter in 1978. The 1986 tax cut reducing the income tax to a modern low of 28 percent was pushed by Sen. Bill Bradley and Rep. Dan Rostenkowski. It won the support of forty-four of forty-seven Democrats in the Senate. Meanwhile, Social Security taxes on working people kept increasing. In 1997, Bill Clinton signed a big cut in the capital gains rate; and in 2010 as part of a budget deal, Obama extended the George W. Bush rate cuts that were set to expire.

Ordinary citizens were not clamoring for any of this. You could understand the voter confusion about which side the Democrats were on. Obama did sign a modestly progressive tax reform in 2012, but Joe Biden is the first president in recent memory to press for significantly higher taxes on the very rich.

In the 2016 backlash against Obama, America's first Black

president, much has been made of race. Racism remains pervasive in America, yet in the 2008 election, Obama looked like an outsider who looked as if he just might bring fundamental change, and he managed to win about 40 percent of the white working-class vote. It was Obama's failure to deliver economic gains for ordinary people and his alliance with Wall Street that allowed white racism once again to fill the political vacuum, setting the table for the Tea Party revolt and Trump.

8

America's Last Chance

America could narrowly escape Trumpism yet again and continue the process of rebuilding a more just society, or we could well lose our democracy for keeps. As this book goes to press in January 2022, I can offer a hopeful scenario and a disastrous one. Let's do the disaster first, then take a deeper look at the hope.

The long-term outlook is far from auspicious. Climate change is upon us, earlier than the most pessimistic forecasts. Dislocations are inevitable. This leads to unhappy citizens and difficult policy choices. It requires even more expenditure of public funds to prevent even worse outcomes, diverting money from more visible and popular uses. If the New Deal proposition is that government can be effective in solving problems and helping ordinary people, climate change makes that harder to pull off, because worsened climate events are baked in for years to come. Even if Biden does everything right, the everyday experience of extreme climate events will intensify.

For at least a century, the normal pattern for the president's party has been to lose House and Senate seats in mid-term elections, even without a deliberate assault on the right to vote. The three exceptions are FDR in 1934, Bill Clinton in 1998, and George W. Bush in 2002. Each of these is instructive. The Democrats gained seats in 1934 because FDR had delivered practical help and restored a sense of possibility. The midterm election in a president's sixth year is usually particularly bad for incumbents, but Clinton's party gained in 1998, because Republicans overreached with impeachment. And Republicans gained in 2002 after the sense of national unity following the attacks of September 11, 2001. Can any of these be a precedent?

Biden has certainly provided concrete benefits, as FDR did. The problem is that America is so badly divided that practical help makes only modest inroads in Republican tribal loyalty. Polls show extensive public support for the elements of Biden's Build Back Better program, but little of that support has rubbed off on Biden personally.

Historical comparisons also suggest a rough correlation between a president's net approval rating several months before a midterm election and how well his party does. Biden's has been in the range that could cost the Democrats control of Congress. Based on past patterns, the Democrats could be headed for loss of forty to fifty House seats. Biden and the Democrats have also been damaged by the outbreak of inflation, even though it is mostly the result of supply chain bottlenecks and not Biden's policies. Republican gerrymandering will cost Democrats five or more House seats, and voter suppression even more. In a typical midterm, especially after the election of a new president, the supporters of the party that lost are more highly energized than the new president's backers who are more complacent. This seems to have been foreshadowed in the off-off-year elections of November 2021.

If Democrats do lose even one house of Congress, escalating Republican anti-democratic behavior suggests the kind of retribution that could occur. Progressive Democrats could be censured or expelled from the House or denied committee seats on one pretext or another. The loss of either house in 2022 could also make it easier for Republicans to steal the presidential election in 2024. A legal memo to Donald Trump by attorney John

Eastman, disclosed in Bob Woodward and Robert Costa's book *Peril*, provides a cynical playbook whose strategies will again be available in 2024. Several Republican-controlled states could certify electors who would reverse the actual results of the election.* If that occurs, either the election will be stolen outright, or the final result will be thrown to the House or decided by a partisan Supreme Court. If a Republican Congress is fraudulently elected in 2022, leading to a Republican president installed in 2024, voter suppression will deepen and America effectively ceases to be a democracy.

A further potential trap for Democrats is the issue of whether Biden runs in 2024. If Democrats do lose one or both houses of Congress, there will be immense pressure on Biden to step aside. Even if Democrats keep Congress, many will say that Biden, at eighty-two, is too old to seek a second term. But the approval ratings of his vice president, Kamala Harris, are consistently lower than Biden's. There is a risk of a free-for-all contest for the 2024 Democratic nomination, at a time when Democrats need nothing so much as unity.

So, where's the hopeful scenario?

The first thing to appreciate is that the 2022 election is anything but a normal midterm. Democrats will have one not-so-secret weapon that was not available last Election Day—Donald Trump.

Trump was mostly offstage in late 2021, but he will be floridly present as the 2022 election approaches, dividing his party, reminding Democrats and independents just how crazy and dangerous he was as president, and why they turned out in unprecedented numbers in both 2018 and 2020. Trump will still

---

* Three conservative Supreme Court justices called attention to this option in their separate opinion in the 2000 *Bush v. Gore* ruling.

be obsessing about the "stolen" 2020 election and attacking Republicans who want to change the subject. Trump will not be on the ballot in 2022, but the election can still be a referendum on him and the slavish adherence of most Republican candidates to Trumpism—which does not embody the values of most Americans.

Galvanized by the menace of Trump, alarmed voters turned out in 2018 at record rates for a midterm, flipped forty-one net House seats from Republican to Democrat, and took back the House despite increasing voter suppression in states controlled by Republicans. In 2020, though they did not do as well in the House, they kept the House majority and took back the Senate, and of course ousted Trump from the White House.

Citizens who voted in 2018 and 2020 but not 2016 cast their ballots by a margin of 58 percent for Democrats, far higher than the national average. That includes the 7.7 million registered Democratic voters who skipped 2016, but did turn out in 2018 and 2020, and the 18 million Democrats who cast ballots for the first time in 2020. An even more hopeful harbinger is that those who voted in 2018 but not 2016 supported Biden in 2020 by a resounding margin of 62 to 36. Voters under thirty broke for the Democrats in 2018, 72 to 23.

A key question is whether 2022 will be like 2018. As in 2018, Trump will not be on the ballot, but he will be omnipresent. Republicans will mobilize their base, but it is a smaller core than the Democratic base—if that Democratic base can be motivated to vote. This is why Republicans are so hell-bent on destroying democracy. Fear of Trump helped Biden immensely in 2020. Among voters who had cast ballots in 2016, Biden won by 1.5 percent. But among those voting for the first time in 2020, Biden's margin was 11.7 points. If these citizens and others can be organized to vote given the equally high stakes in 2022, the Democrats can beat the midterm jinx.

My wager is that as we get closer to the November election and as Trump personally looms larger, it will start feeling more like the 2018 midterm. Trump will also help by his campaign of vilification against Republicans in swing districts who are not hard-core MAGA loyalists. He has somehow missed the elementary reality that they need to trim their Trumpism in districts with lots of independents or moderate Republicans in order to get elected.

Trump has been recruiting candidates to challenge Republicans whom he perceives as disloyal. In swing districts, the ouster of a moderate incumbent by a fervent Trumper could flip several seats to Democrats. Of the several dozen House Republicans who refused to join the Trump fanatics in challenging the 2020 presidential election results, thirty-three of them won their own elections by less than 60 percent. All these seats would be vulnerable if a far-right Republican ousted a moderate incumbent in a primary.

As Congressional Republicans become more unhinged and condoning of outright political violence, that will also serve to remind voters of the stakes in the midterm. The election will be nationalized and Republican members of Congress will be yoked to Trump—in a way that does not play to Republican strength. Past patterns, therefore, are of limited value in prognosticating the coming midterm, which is in no way a normal election—just as the Republicans have ceased to be a normal party. If swing voters and dispirited Democrats temporarily overlooked that chilling reality on Election Day 2021, they will soon be reminded.

Many commentators have drawn the wrong lessons from the narrow victory of Glenn Youngkin over Terry McAuliffe in the 2021 election for governor of Virginia. McAuliffe tried to paint Youngkin as a Trump surrogate, in his campaign rhetoric and in crude TV ads that showed Youngkin morphing into Trump. It didn't work. Therefore, say many pundits, it won't work for

Democrats to make 2022 about Trump. That conclusion is profoundly wrong.

First, McAuliffe ran a weak campaign. A former governor who had been out of office for four years, and a close ally of Bill Clinton, he seemed a figure from another era. As a business Democrat, he lacked the populist touch. Youngkin, as an investment banker with a calm persona, looked like a traditional center-right Republican, He was the ideal non-Trump without being anti-Trump. Youngkin also got very lucky in that he avoided a divisive primary, a fracas that would rub raw the divide between the sheer craziness of the Trumpers and the professed moderation of center-right Republicans. Youngkin asked that Trump stay away. Trump did. He will not stay away in 2022.

Youngkin was able to perfect the dog-whistle strategy of posturing moderate while signaling the Trump base that he was one of them. He used a parental complaint from 2013 by a Virginia mother, Laura Murphy, that a Pulitzer Prize–winning Toni Morrison novel, *Beloved*, assigned to a senior AP English class, had upset her teenage son (as such literature is intended to do—shall we ban Hamlet?). In 2015, Republicans had sponsored legislation, popularly called the "Beloved Bill," allowing parents to opt their children out of curricula with "sexually explicit content." As governor, McAuliffe had vetoed the bill. Rehashing this issue gave Youngkin the perfect appeal to racism couched in the language of parents' rights. In a key debate with Youngkin, McAuliffe fell into the trap declaring that parents should not second-guess teachers. Even with all this, Youngkin won by just two points.

A much better example for 2022 of how to hang Trump and Trumpism around the necks of Republican Congressional candidates is what occurred in the attempted California recall election of Governor Gavin Newsom. At the time the recall was launched, at the peak of the pandemic, Newsom had lost a lot of public support. Many voters were aggrieved by school closures, lockdown orders, job losses, and general economic conditions. California has also suffered the effects of fires, droughts, and floods. Voter frustration with Newsom was crystallized by an episode in November 2020 when Newsom, in violation of his own state guidelines, attended a large indoor fancy dinner in wine country, many of whose guests were lobbyists. At one point in the campaign, polls showed that Newsom could well lose.

But then the governor turned the tables on the Trumpers. Unlike McAuliffe, Newsom was lucky in that the candidate positioned to succeed him was a far-right Trumper talk show host named Larry Elder. So Newsom's entire theme became: if you want California to look like Trumpland, vote for the recall. California's progressive base went all out to produce a large turnout, something that is difficult in a special election. In the end, Newsom defeated the recall, 62–38, with a stunning turnout of over 58 percent. It was the identical margin by which he had been elected governor in 2018.

You might say that not every Democratic candidate will have a crackpot opponent like Larry Elder as a foil. But they will have Donald Trump, who is every bit as much a crackpot as Elder and far more dangerous, as we saw during his presidency and his efforts to overthrow the 2020 election. So yes, Democrats do need to nationalize the 2022 election and make it about Trump and Trumpism. Strategists who say otherwise should find another profession.

The larger moral of this story is that Democrats at all levels need to work harder to define issues and Republicans, and not let Republicans define them. Most pocketbook issues, accurately framed, play to Democratic strength.

Biden's personal approval ratings may be down, but the details of Biden's three major legislative programs are highly popular. According to polls conducted at the time Build Back Better passed the House on November 19, 2021, 88 percent of Americans supported Build Back Better's measures to cut prescription drug prices; 84 percent supported the provisions to lower health insurance premiums; 73 percent favored the funding for paid family leave; 72 percent of Americans backed Build Back Better's creation of clean energy jobs to combat climate change; and 67 percent of Americans supported the funding for universal pre-kindergarten.

Democratic candidates should be reminding voters that all of this will be at risk if Republicans take back either house of Congress; and that Democrats can complete the unfinished business of Build Back Better if they can increase their majority.

Republican missteps are likely to help Democrats in other ways. Governor Ron DeSantis may be able to make an anti-vax alliance work in Florida (where he is usefully splitting the Trump coalition), but as the broader public grows increasingly weary of Covid upsurges, these tactics and messages are increasingly toxic outside hard-core Trump country. About 65 percent of Americans support a universal vaccine mandate. As more people get vaccinated and Covid doesn't quite go away largely because of people who refuse vaccination, Democratic candidates can remind voters elsewhere that fringe, anti-science, and anti–public health policies are likely to become national law if Republicans take control of Congress.

Another blunder is the Republican overreach on reproductive rights. For decades, Republicans have been able to play a game of pretending to uphold *Roe v. Wade* in principle while destroying it in practice. The Texas law, defining fetal viability as six weeks, ends that charade. Polls show that most voters oppose it, and the issue will be especially toxic for Republicans among suburban women, who are key to many swing districts. The *Wall Street Journal*, in a livid editorial, accused the sponsors of the Texas abortion law of "handing Democrats a political grenade."

Looking at the Senate, the odds seem decent that Democrats will hold on to their bare working majority, and maybe even pick up a seat or two. Of the seats defended by Democrats, three or four are vulnerable. In Georgia, Raphael Warnock must defend the seat he won in a special election in 2020. In New Hampshire, incumbent Democrat Maggie Hassan is potentially at risk, though she dodged a bullet when her strongest potential opponent, Governor Chris Sununu, passed up the Senate race. Mark Kelly in Arizona and Catherine Cortez Masto in Nevada, two blue-trending states, might also be vulnerable, but less so. Other incumbents seem reasonably safe.

Offsetting possible Democratic losses, at least four Democratic pickups seem possible. In Pennsylvania, which voted for Biden in 2020, a Democrat will contest an open seat with the retirement of Republican Pat Toomey. In Wisconsin, also carried by Biden, the far-right incumbent, Ron Johnson, will likely face a strong challenge. In North Carolina, a competitive state with a Democratic governor, the incumbent Republican senator, Richard Burr, is also retiring. In Missouri, Republican incumbent Roy Blunt barely won the seat in 2016. Blunt is retiring, and the leading contender for the Republican nomination is Eric Greitens, who resigned as governor after a woman with whom he had an extramarital affair raised accusations of abuse. Democrats also have a strong candidate in Tim Ryan in Ohio, where a Republican retirement opens a seat. It is too early to handicap these races, but a net Democratic gain of one or even two seems possible.

At this writing, plans are being laid for a Democracy Summer 2022, with massive efforts at voter registration and organizing. Given the ever more extreme Republican tactics to suppress voting, intimidate poll workers, and change counts after the fact, plus a new wave of gerrymandering and the failure of Congress to pass voting rights legislation, you might think that suppression will beat mobilization. But if you take closer look, there are at least thirty swing seats in states that have fair voting systems. And even in Republican-controlled states, the tactic of packing Democratic voters into a few overwhelmingly Democratic seats means that those seats are protected against suppression tactics. Without suppression and gerrymandering, Democrats would win ten to twenty more seats. To offset this tilt, the Democratic mobilization needs to be even larger—as it was in 2018.

Biden's basic challenge is to use his accomplishments and the practical help they have delivered to ordinary Americans as a strategy for assembling a new majority governing coalition. This will not be easy because of the irrational support of so many white working-class voters for a party and a leader in Donald Trump that plainly do not serve their pocketbook interests.

The historian and essayist Thomas Frank offers a useful guide to this dilemma. In his influential 2004 book, *What's the Matter with Kansas?*, Frank argued that many working-class people voted for Republicans, against their own economic interests, because cultural issues—the famous trilogy of guns, God, and gays, as well as racism—were crowding out economic ones. But Frank's premise was that Democrats served the interests of working people. By the time he wrote a sequel, *Listen, Liberal* (2016), Frank had appropriately revised his view. It wasn't that culture trumped economics; *it was that Democratic presidents had switched sides*. Neoliberal Democrats like the Clintons and Obama had basically stopped serving working families in favor of serving Wall Street, so they made the job of fake populists who were cultural reactionaries that much easier.

Here is where Biden is far better positioned than Hillary Clinton or Barack Obama to win back at least some Trump voters. But this project will take more than two years. FDR, after all, governed for twelve years. Many of Roosevelt's accomplishments, such as finally ending the Great Depression, required the even greater national mobilization of World War II. Biden needs to retain and increase his governing majority in 2022 because there is so much yet to be done.

Some of what needs to be done can be achieved by executive orders, progressive appointees, and expansive use of existing laws. One of Biden's more far-reaching orders, issued on February 24, 2021, directed the National Security Council and the National Economic Council to coordinate a government-wide assessment and strategy on supply chains and industrial policy, and to issue a comprehensive report within a hundred days. The 250-page report that resulted, the superb work of four cabinet departments, is the most impressive economic planning document since World War II.

The order, and the thinking behind the report, jettisons the economic wisdom that was conventional from Carter to Obama—that government is not competent to "pick winners." Given the threats to American national security and manufacturing from unreliable global supply chains, thrown into relief by the pandemic, the United States has no choice but to determine which sectors, technologies, end products, and inputs need to be made at home and how vital technologies should be kept from geopolitical adversaries such as China that play by different rules. The report, issued in June 2021, includes detailed strategy and policy assessments on how the United States can gain greater economic security and technological leadership in semiconductors, large-capacity storage batteries essential for a green energy conversion, materials for domestic production of pharmaceuticals, and critical materials needed for the national defense. This strategy also promotes domestic jobs.

The supply chain crisis, which is the source of most of the recent bout of inflation, is the legacy of three perverse policies of neoliberalism—just-in-time production, hyper-globalization, and deregulation. In the late 1970s, it became fashionable for companies to keep inventories low to save money. To cut costs further, they used far-flung global sources of supply, relying on countries with cheap, oppressed labor and weak or nonexistent regulation. Economists praised the greater efficiency—and ignored the increased systemic fragility.

These corporate practices then combined with deregulation of every major industry that made up the supply chain—ports, ocean shipping, trucking, and rail. The nation's logistics system was privatized; there was no attention to it, as a system. The increased economic concentration that resulted led to even less attention to whether there was enough slack in the system.

The consequence was ever larger container ships that could be accommodated in fewer and fewer ports; a shift of trucking from a good salaried and unionized job to the underpaid casual work of independent contractors. That in turn created a long-term shortage of truck drivers, something unheard of when truckers had decent pay. Deregulated rail meant that rail companies were free to sell off rail yards to real estate developers, reducing needed rail capacity for offloading containers. Deregulated ports meant that a cartel of eight giant shipping companies, none of them U.S.-owned, dictated shipping policies for their own profit, operating vessels with too many containers to be unloaded at most ports, and prolonging the unloading process; large retailers used scarce port terminal space to store inventory, further clogging the process of unloading and transshipping cargo.

All the major deregulation laws were enacted by Democratic presidents, at the behest of conservative economic advisers and powerful corporate interests. Once again, Biden is paying for the sins of his predecessors. He is the first president who is serious about rebuilding a national logistics system, as well as doing what he can to improve the supply chain mess in the near term, and reclaiming domestic production.

Biden also gets related credit for reversing America's China policy. To the shame of both Republican presidents Bush, as well as Democrats Clinton and Obama, American policy made the wishful assumption that if we admitted China to the global trading system with only the gentlest of quid pro quos, China would inexorably evolve into a capitalist democracy that played by the rules, and our trade deficit would move toward balance. In the years since China was admitted into the World Trade Organization, China has only become more of a mercantilist economy, run by an increasingly Leninist Communist Party. America's trade deficit has quintupled.

It fell to Trump to pursue a tougher China policy. But Trump's version was an incoherent blend of tariffs and bluster, with no complementary domestic industrial policy. Biden has married a firmer stance on China's illicit economic practices with a comprehensive strategy for restoring domestic industry and supply chains—and without provoking a military confrontation. This is a fine case of the creative use of a president's executive policy, and one of the few areas that attracts substantial Republican support.

Another of Biden's early actions was an executive order issued on April 27, 2021, requiring any company that bids on a federal contract to pay its workers a minimum wage of at least $15 an hour. The preexisting Obama order, from 2014, set the minimum at $10.10. In the context of tightening labor markets, this order will have spillover effects raising other wages.

A more comprehensive example is the order Biden issued on July 9, 2021, on economic concentration and competition policy. The Biden order includes seventy-two separate initiatives to be carried out by more than a dozen government agencies. The order begins with an analysis of how the extreme economic concentration in industry after industry costs consumers in the form of higher prices and fewer choices, retards innovation, and gives employers increased power to deny workers good wages. This framing alone is revolutionary. Ever since Ronald Reagan appointed Robert Bork to dismantle antitrust policy, government has not used the powers it has because the two agencies charged with carrying out the antitrust laws, the Federal Trade Commission and the Department of Justice, basically agreed with Bork.

Until Biden's chair of the Federal Trade Commission, Lina Khan, wrote her groundbreaking 2017 article for the *Yale Law Journal*, the conventional wisdom was that the big platform monopolies like Google, Facebook, and Amazon could go on buying up or destroying potential rivals with impunity, and using their access to customer data to undercut competitors who used their platforms in their marketing. Khan demonstrated how existing antitrust law could be applied to platform monopolies.

The remedies in the executive order are a reflection of just how extreme the abuses have become, and how radical Biden is compared to his recent Democratic predecessors. In their substance, these proposals are not radical in the sense of being far left. They are simply about making capitalism work as advertised. This is just the beginning of a long road back to an economy of better balance between corporations, workers, and consumers.

For example, the order bans non-compete clauses as a condition of employment. These requirements make it much more difficult for workers to shop around for better offers and be paid what they are worth in the marketplace. Research shows that non-compete clauses cost workers an estimated 17 percent in their earnings.

The order goes after abuses that are vivid and costly to consumers such as price-gouging on hearing aids. It has long been an open secret that for most hearing-impaired people, low-cost hearing aids work about as well as far more expensive and profitable products made by large medical device companies. These hearing aids cost an average of $5,000 and are often not covered by insurance. The Biden order requires low-cost hearing aids to be available over the counter at drugstores.

The order also bars manufacturers of products like cars and farm machinery from prohibiting users from doing their own repairs. It has long been a mark of self-respect on the part of farmers and working-class people that they are able to fix their own cars, trucks, or tractors. Lately, as vehicles have become more computerized, manufacturers have locked access to onboard computers and required purchasers to get all their repairs at licensed dealers, at far greater expense. Even before the order was finalized, Apple and Microsoft changed their policies and now allow consumers to repair their products wherever they like, saving costs.

FDR's administration increased antitrust enforcement eightfold. Biden's speech introducing the competition order was the most important presidential statement on concentration and competition since Roosevelt. "Capitalism without competition isn't capitalism," he said. "It's exploitation." Biden quoted FDR's call for an economic bill of rights, citing Roosevelt's goal of ensuring the "right of every businessman, large and small, to trade in an atmosphere of freedom from unfair competition and domination by monopolies at home or abroad."

To review the order in detail is to take a guided tour of the abuses of today's capitalism. This order is especially valuable politically—if Biden is able to combine it with public education. Much of what government does is esoteric and technical. But these policies and the abuses they remedy are clear and simple. People know if they have to pay a king's ransom for a hearing aid, or if they are prohibited from working on their cars. These policies benefit ordinary people directly, often the very sorts of people inclined to take Fox News as gospel and vote for Donald Trump. The details of the competition order will be fought by the powerful corporations that benefit from the status quo, and this conflict can be a useful political economy lesson demonstrating to citizens who their real enemies are and what it's like to have a government on their side—pure FDR and Give 'Em Hell Harry. Biden needs to do better at getting the word out on all the ways his program helps ordinary Americans.

Happily, antitrust is one of the few areas of partial bipartisan collaboration. Democrats don't like the economic concentration because of the harm to consumers and workers. Some Republicans actually believe in capitalism as it is supposed to be practiced. Other Republicans want to punish the social liberalism of Silicon Valley and the habit of tech billionaires of supporting Democrats. A package of bipartisan antitrust bills, strengthening the criteria for breaking up monopoly power, is moving through Congress.

Some necessary reforms, which are essential but less vivid to the lay public, are also well within the administrative capacity of agencies. A contributing cause to the collapse of 2008 was the corruption of auditors. The Dodd-Frank Act authorizes the SEC to require one very simple remedy. Auditors hired by corporations would have to rotate, so that there would be no incentive for accounting firms to soft-pedal findings in the hope of getting repeat business. The SEC could implement this by regulation.

The SEC could also institute a requirement that stock brokerages executing orders for investors give them the best available price, under penalty of criminal prosecution for fraud. This would end the several versions of the abuse known as "front-running," in which the brokerage delays completing the transaction ordered by the customer until it can place its own bets based on knowledge of pending customer trades. This is another conflict of interest between broker and the investing public anticipated by FDR.

The SEC and the bank regulatory agencies have the power to

make referrals for criminal prosecutions. Despite the legal con-
ceit that corporations are people, we know that the real people
are the overpaid executives who run banks and devise corrupt
policies that harm consumers. As recently as the savings and loan
scandal of the late 1980s (but not in the much more damaging
and deeply corrupt 2008 general collapse), hundreds of executives went to jail. If bank officials know they face prison time for
illegal acts, that would be more a powerful deterrent than scads
of new regulations.

Today, many of the practices that crashed the economy in
2008 have crept back into the banking system. Collateralized
debt obligations (CDOs), the complex securities backed by subprime mortgages, fell out of favor after the great collapse. But
in recent years, investment bankers reinvented them as CLOs,
which stands for collateralized loan obligations. It's the same
beast, under a different name. The only difference is that CLOs
tend to be backed by business loans—subprime loans to businesses that are too risky to sell bonds directly to investors or
get conventional bank financing. According to Professor Frank
Partnoy, as of the end of 2020 there were more than a trillion
dollars' worth of CLOs outstanding, slightly larger than the
CDO market at the time of the 2008 crash. Partnoy found that
for the thirty largest "global systemically important banks," the
typical exposure to CLOs and similar very highly leveraged loans
was about 60 percent of their capital. So even after Dodd-Frank,
abuses similar to those that caused the 2008 crash continue.

What's needed is far more fundamental reform of the financial system, to break up both financial concentration and concentrated risk. A decade after the cleanup of the great collapse, the
big banks have more market share than ever. The Dodd-Frank
reforms served mainly to give the banks more of a cushion to enable them to make lucrative and speculative investments, with

less risk of a systemic meltdown. A lot of financial reform could be accomplished with tougher enforcement, but some of it will take legislation.

Private equity, as noted in chapter 7, is one of the most predatory abuses of American capitalism. Elizabeth Warren has offered a bill that would put an end to the looting and much of private equity's business model. Among other provisions, Warren's Stop Wall Street Looting Act would drastically limit the tax deductibility of debt used to acquire companies and require the private equity partners to share responsibility for the debt. It would ban the payment of "special dividends" for two years after an acquisition and would make it much harder for firms to loot worker pensions by giving priority to worker pay and pensions in any bankruptcy process.

The bottom line is that the economy performed just fine before the invention of private equity. It was another of those financial "innovations" that served only the financial engineers and harmed everyone else. (Private equity should not be confused with venture capital, which has its own problems, but at least venture capitalists put their own resources into actual ventures rather than taking money out.)

Another Warren bill, the Accountable Capitalism Act, would revive and modernize a proposal first made during the Progressive Era by requiring all corporations with over a billion dollars in sales to get a federal charter. That charter, in turn, would require that workers elect 40 percent of directors, and that all political spending by corporations be approved by 75 percent of the corporate board.

One more Warren proposal would extend the long-standing principle of common carriage to the giant tech platform monopolies. Any platform with global annual revenue of greater than $25 billion would be designated as a platform utility. Rather in the same way that FDR's Glass-Steagall Act forced banks to become either commercial banks or investment banks, Warren's plan would compel large tech companies to either provide internet search services or offer products over the internet, but not both. Google and Amazon are extreme examples of how tech platforms that do both things have conflicts of interest at the expense of their competitors and the public.

The gross inequality in today's economy is one part the result of the hyper-concentration of capital, and one part the consequence of the steady weakening of labor. We need to reverse these trends on both sides of the equation. There is a good deal that Biden's Labor Department and the White House can accomplish by executive action, including cracking down on abuses of misclassification of payroll employees as gig workers, and holding parent companies responsible for the actions of their contractors and franchisees. But a real re-balancing of power will require a stronger labor movement. Biden, much more than his recent Democratic predecessors, supports tough labor law reform. The PRO Act, which stands for Protecting the Right to Organize, would go beyond other recent (and failed) reform proposals authorizing representation elections once a majority of workers in a potential local had signed union cards. The PRO Act would restore the original provisions of the Wagner Act and strictly prohibit management from propagandizing in elections for union representation.

These several legislative proposals and Biden executive orders can begin to restore the kind of balance in the economy that was Roosevelt's legacy—an economy with greater equity between labor and capital, and between the public sector and the private. To the extent that much of the economy is privately owned, reforms like these insist that the market part of the economy operate the way it allegedly operates in a textbook—without monopoly abuses, conflicts of interests, or perverse incentives like those of private equity where investors profit by running companies they have acquired into the ground. It also means a banking system that is servant of the real economy rather than master, one that is decentralized enough that the failure of one bank does not crash the whole system, and simple in its fundamentals so that it is transparent enough to regulate.

Biden has used executive power to postpone student debt repayment. He could cancel that debt entirely. He has the power to put drug patents into the public domain, cutting consumer costs. A few such actions would demonstrate leadership, deliver practical help, and put the president squarely on the side of the people.

Government needs to take another leaf from the FDR playbook and resume doing more things directly, through public institutions. Regulation can take you only so far when private players with grossly concentrated wealth exercise so much political influence. They use this influence both to weaken reform legislation and then to pursue a strategy of trench warfare to undermine its enforcement. In the case of the Obama Affordable Care Act, progressives fought and ultimately lost a struggle to have a "public option" available to every citizen who used the ACA. In addition to a choice of private insurance plans, with a public option you could opt into Medicare or something very much like it. The insurance industry recognized the mortal threat and forced Obama to dump the public option.

But more public options are precisely what we need. The votes are not there for Medicare for All. However, as part of a radically incremental strategy of gradually moving to universal public health insurance, we could begin with public options for all people under sixty-five. During the 2020 primary season, Pete Buttigieg, punning on Bernie Sanders's plan, proposed "Medicare for All Who Want It." Since Medicare is more reliable and cost-effective than any private competitor, this would gradually crowd out private insurance. The idea evokes FDR.

Roosevelt advocated public electric power, in a wonderfully Rooseveltian phrase, as "yardstick competition" in which government competes directly with the private sector. Government-run power companies could demonstrate just how cheaply and efficiently electricity could be supplied. This accomplished two things. As a teachable moment at the level of ideology, yardstick competition turned on its head the conservative assumption that markets are more efficient than government. And as a practical matter, the competition of public power forced private suppliers to lower their prices.

Today, government could directly supply much cheaper universal broadband. In Chattanooga, Tennessee, in TVA territory, the locally owned public power company offers residents an ultra-high-speed internet package that is faster and cheaper than anything offered by commercial telecom or cable companies. For $67.99 a month, you can get internet, phone, and cable TV with ultra-fast 1-gig broadband. The very high-speed internet, available at speeds up to 10 gigabytes per second, has also served Chattanooga as an economic development strategy, enabling the city to attract tech companies that require advanced broadband.

Commercial rivals, recognizing the threat, successfully lobbied the state legislature to prohibit the local public power company from offering its package outside the city limits. As part of Biden's infrastructure initiative, government could dramatically expand public broadband, not just for underserved areas but for the public generally. This of course will require a political battle royal with private industry. Biden's infrastructure program provides billions in grants to the states to expand broadband but is agnostic on whether the providers should be public or private. They should be public, and Biden needs to rally public sentiment and make this a political issue and a teachable moment. (Note to Biden's communications team: Bring the president to Chattanooga; have him appear with satisfied local citizens; and explain to the rest of America that this could be yours but for greedy private power, cable, and telecom companies. Find an FDR anniversary to invoke. Film it for TV spots.)

Some public options require legislation; others can be done by executive order. One of the worst abuses in the privatization of public functions has been the proliferation of private prisons. These companies, typically owned by private equity, make their profits by running prisons that are even worse than their lamentable public counterparts, with worse food and medical care, exorbitant charges for inmate phone calls, and fewer well-trained, professionalized, or decently paid guards. Privatized prisons also create a buffer layer to undercut public accountability. After multiple prison scandals, Biden in one of his first executive orders issued January 26, 2021, required the Justice Department to let all contracts with private prison companies expire and not to renew them. At this writing, the order has not been extended to ICE detention facilities, 72 percent of which are operated by private contractors and are a well-documented disgrace. This prohibition could also be extended to all state and local governments that get federal funds.

Another promising area for a public option is postal banking. Postal banking was initiated in Britain in 1861 and was long part of the progressive agenda. In the United States, it was authorized in 1910 after the financial panic of 1907, and the Post Office offered basic banking services between 1911 and 1967. Nonprofit credit unions and savings and loans also used to be a much larger part of the consumer financial sector. Given how abusive commercial banks have become to consumers, and the large number of poor people who are "unbanked," relying on check-cashing services, payday lenders, and private remittance services, this is a gap that could again be filled by the Postal Service. There is currently a small pilot program of postal banking in a few communities. The Postal Service, whose head, Louis DeJoy, is a holdover Trump appointee, doesn't believe in it and has done little to make it work.

When it comes to social policy, direct public provision is often superior to the widely touted alternative of vouchers. The trouble with vouchers is that a lot of the taxpayer money leaks into the pockets of for-profit players. A striking example is so-called Section 8 vouchers for housing. Landlords fill unattractive rental properties with Section 8 tenants. Then, when a neighborhood is gentrified, up goes the rent and out goes the tenant. We need to revive socially owned housing, including public housing, limited-equity co-ops, and community land trusts, forever insulated from market pressures in real estate.

Childcare and early childhood education are another area where true public institutions, modeled on public kindergartens, do a far better job than the current patchwork of for-profit providers, often financed by vouchers or tax credits with far too little quality control. Head Start, a fully public program, outperforms any of these. The state-of-the-art system for early childhood education and day care is sponsored by the Defense Department for service men and women, with costs on an affordable sliding scale, and well-compensated professional teachers rather than glorified babysitters who are underqualified and underpaid. Biden's expansion of early childhood and day care financing under his human infrastructure plan is a good start, but it keeps some of the patchwork. The goal should be a comprehensive system built around public school systems.

By the same token, the repeated scandals involving deceptive proprietary trade schools and for-profit colleges, substantially supported by federally guaranteed student loans, demonstrate that public community colleges are a far more honest and cost-effective use of public money. Biden needs to use his bully pulpit to connect these dots and connect them to people's lives: public is often far better than private.

Ever since Nixon's Southern Strategy, Republicans have succeeded all too well at stoking racism as a way of diverting voter attention from common economic interests. It's a very old tactic. Martin Luther King Jr. explained it as well as anyone, in his speech at the conclusion of the 1965 Selma to Montgomery march. Speaking from the Alabama Capitol steps, Dr. King said: "The southern aristocracy took the world and gave the poor white man Jim Crow. And when his wrinkled stomach cried out for the food that his empty pockets could not provide, he ate Jim Crow, a psychological bird that told him that no matter how bad off he was, at least he was a white man, better than the black man."

A pioneering project called the Race-Class Narrative tested a variety of progressive messages, comparing those that ducked race and just talked about common class interests with those that explicitly mentioned race. The idea was to make clear Dr. King's point—that racist policies also were harmful to whites. Researchers found that race-class approaches that acknowledged the special challenges of race "were more convincing than color-blind economic populism." Three-quarters of respondents in a multiracial group agreed with the statement, "Instead of delivering for working people, politicians hand kickbacks to their donors who send jobs overseas. They then turn around and blame new immigrants or people of color, to divide and distract us from the real source of our problems."

Heather McGhee, one of the creators of the Race-Class Narrative, demonstrated the power of common interests in her recent book, *The Sum of Us*. In the era when the federal government was at last requiring integration of public facilities under the 1964 Civil Rights Act, city after city in the Deep South paved over public swimming pools and closed public parks rather than having to witness whites sharing recreation facilities. Whites and Blacks sweltered together. Montgomery even closed the public zoo.

It's a very old story. McGhee quotes Hinton Helper, a white Southerner who wrote a book in 1857 tallying all the ways that the planter class that governed the South shortchanged ordinary whites. Pennsylvania, Helper reported, had 393 public libraries; South Carolina, 26. New Hampshire had 2,381 public schools; Mississippi, 782. Plantation owners had a captive free labor force. They didn't need or want educated whites. The poorest, least-educated states and those with the most threadbare public services are still those in the South. Nationally, policies aimed to hurt Blacks also short-change whites. In the recent financial collapse, Blacks were disproportionate targets of subprime scams, but whites suffered right along with them.

Elites have played off Blacks against working whites since slavery times. Fashioning a coalition of common interest, at long last, will be far from easy. Neither Lincoln, nor FDR, nor LBJ could achieve it. Since Johnson, the white working-class mistrust of liberals has only grown, as have legitimate Black demands for overdue justice, some of which scare off white moderates.

The syndrome of violence by police and by white vigilantes against Blacks creates a dynamic that Republicans exploit. When Black citizens and their white allies protest and demand justice, Republicans caricature the demands as "woke," pretending that radical slogans like Defund the Police represent the views of mainstream Democrats, and claiming that abstruse academic concepts like Critical Race Theory are being used in classrooms to brainwash white children. Biden is then caught between the need to reassure his Black supporters that he is working to remedy their grievances, but without providing more ammunition to the right.

When Kyle Rittenhouse was acquitted of all charges, Biden tried to walk that tightrope. He issued a bland statement that seemed to emphasize the importance at keeping protest peaceful more than outrage at the verdict. It began: "While the verdict in Kenosha will leave many Americans feeling angry and concerned, myself included, we must acknowledge that the jury has spoken. I ran on a promise to bring Americans together, because I believe that what unites us is far greater than what divides us." This tepid criticism only further enflamed many Blacks without weakening Republican strategy. Colorado Republican Representative Lauren Boebert tweeted: "It seems liberals want self-defense to be illegal. Try running on that in 2022 and see how far it gets you with the majority of the sane American public."

But the good news is that most of the white American public is less racist than Republicans would like to believe. After the police murder of George Floyd, two-thirds of Americans approved of the Movement for Black Lives. That approval has declined some, but has stabilized at around 55 percent. After former Minneapolis police officer Derek Chauvin was convicted of Floyd's murder in May 2021, three-quarters of Americans approved of the verdict. In November, polls showed that a majority disapproved of the verdict letting the murderous vigilante Kyle Rittenhouse go free.

Biden's presidency will depend on making progress on cross-racial alliances and disarming crude Republican strategies to use violence against Blacks to heighten divisiveness. There are policy initiatives that can accomplish this. In more than a hundred cities, programs divert most 911 calls involving domestic disputes from police responses to EMTs and mental health workers. The results have shown a marked decline in police interventions making matters worse, and happier outcomes. This is a constructive strategy of shifting police resources minus inflammatory slogans like Defund the Police.

The long-term electoral news is also heartening—if Democrats keep playing to strength. The Democrats' 2020 success in Georgia was built on a ten-year organizing campaign led by the very impressive Stacey Abrams. Much of the leadership and the target population were African American, but the coalition and the voters it reached included plenty of white people. About 30 percent of whites voted for Biden, and whites were willing to vote for a Black man for the Senate by a slightly larger percentage. Indeed, the winning margin of Rev. Raphael Warnock, pastor of the Ebenezer Baptist Church once led by Dr. Martin Luther King Jr., exceeded that of the white Democratic Senate candidate on the ballot, Jon Ossoff.

In 2018, in districts north and south with very small Black populations, white voters were willing to elect Black candidates with a compelling pocketbook message. In Newt Gingrich's old district, Georgia's Sixth, which is just 13 percent African American, a Black Democrat, Lucy McBath, took the seat. In Dallas, Colin Allred, a Black civil rights activist and former NFL player, won an upset and took a district where Blacks make up 11 percent of the population. And in the Chicago far western suburbs, in a seat that is 3 percent African American, a thirty-two-year-old Black nurse named Lauren Underwood took a district that was not even on the national Democratic Party map. A Republican stronghold longer than anyone could remember, the seat had once been held by House Speaker Dennis Hastert.

All of these candidates built their campaign around kitchen-table economics—health care, Social Security, jobs, and wages. All were reelected in 2020. Their success, in overwhelmingly white districts, suggests that with credible citizen-politicians reframing public conversations, our country just might begin to transcend its racist legacy and begin to focus on common interests.

When Franklin Roosevelt took office in March 1933, his greatest challenge was to restore hope. So it is with Joe Biden. In the early months of his presidency, Biden did well at rekindling hope and identifying the Democrats' program with popular anxieties and aspirations. This book has argued that Biden can get this spirit back, and that American democracy literally depends on his success.

Roosevelt spoke of transcending fear—"fear itself—nameless, unreasoning, unjustified terror which paralyzes needed efforts to convert retreat into advance." Today's fear is very different from the unreasoning and unjustified fear that Roosevelt sought to dissipate. Our own fears are all too justified. The Republican Party has literally become the party of fear—of domestic terrorism, of hatred, of deceit, of division, and of ending the American experiment in democracy.

Our democracy has been softened up for this final assault for decades, by the substitution of money for broad participation, by assaults on the fundamental right to vote that began with repression of the Black franchise and then in the last decade became general. Our democracy has been weakened by the extreme use of gerrymanders, by the filibuster, by social media as a vehicle for systematic lies, and by ultra-partisan discipline on the part of the Republicans. All of this became more explicit and more extreme after 2016.

There is a naive argument among some political scientists that the degradation of democracy has been symmetrical—an unfortunate polarization and a shift away from constructive bipartisanship. But with the exception of many Democrats' coziness with big money, virtually all of the explicit assaults on democracy itself have been the work of Republicans.

And while a hard-core base of as much as 40 percent of Americans is currently in the Trump camp, the sheer lunacy of the Republicans in Congress and the cynical extremism of Republicans in many states does not have majority support. As details of the attempted coup of January 6, 2021, became public, along with defense of them by nearly all Republicans now in Congress, most Americans recoiled. Polls showed that about two-thirds of all voters were upset or appalled by the insurrection and by the efforts of Republicans in Congress to defend it. Polls also showed that large majorities of Americans want to keep *Roe v. Wade* and a woman's basic right to control her body. As noted, polls demonstrate that most Americans favor specific elements of Biden's Build Back Better program.

All this creates huge opportunities next November for Democratic House and Senate candidates to link these unpopular and often insane beliefs and actions directly to their Republican opponents. Do you want vigilante justice and government by insurrection? Vote for my opponent. Do you want abortion restrictions in our state to look like those of Mississippi and Texas? Vote for my opponent. Tired of the child tax credit, improved roads, bridges, and transit, and more affordable health care? Vote for my opponent. And how about another term for Donald Trump, probably stolen? Be my guest. And—evoking Truman—don't vote for me, vote for yourselves.

Biden does not have FDR's intuitive eloquence, but Biden will not be on the ballot in 2022. And in effect Trump will. And while one can criticize Biden's "messaging," it is far from easy to build a simple message, say, around the reality that today's inflation is mainly the result of a supply chain mess that in turn is the result of four decades of deregulation coupled with corporate opportunism. The right, by contrast, can do simple messages not inconvenienced by fact, nuance, or complexity.

The political reality today is that there are dozens of swing districts but few swing voters. The outcome in 2022 will depend entirely on turnout. The hard-core Trump base will turn out. The survival of our democracy depends on whether Democrats and Democrat-leaning independents turn out. Here, America's young are key. In 2018 and again in 2020, voters under thirty went heavily for Biden. The young have every reason to be fearful, even cynical. They face a future of worsening climate change and ever higher barriers of entry into the middle class. My bet is that Democrats will persuade the young that their future will be even grimmer if the far right takes over America, and that 2022 will see a bumper turnout.

At stake is not just the defense and advance of democracy but the use of that democracy to serve the common people. As we have lost the latter, we are now in danger of losing the former. Biden, evoking Roosevelt, deserves our gratitude for seeing the connection between political democracy and a just economy, and for going big. One has to hope that if he and the Democrats can succeed, the appeal of American fascism will gradually begin to recede.

To say that all this is a long-term project is the mother of understatements. A good shorthand for what we are trying to recover is the Enlightenment—the ancient argument of reason versus blind faith. It dates to Galileo versus the Church, Copernicus versus Ptolemy, and modernity versus the Salem witch trials. One of America's founding myths is the idea of progress. But we have learned from our brush with fascism that history does not move in one direction. Dark eras of regression can last for decades, even centuries.

America has never been more in need of smart, enlightened, compelling leadership. There is so much reason to despair, but there are grounds for hope. To be hopeful is not to be wishful. We need to invoke what is best in America—and be smarter and more strategic than those who invoke the worst.

Acknowledgments

I'd like to acknowledge by name all of the Biden administration people who spoke to me on background. But that would violate the rules. You know who you are, and thank you.

The people who I can acknowledge begin with Elizabeth Warren and her senior staff. The program that Joe Biden is carrying out, of profound reform of corrupted capitalism, is fundamentally Warren's. It is the public philosophy she would have pursued had she been the Democratic nominee and current president. She, more than any other person, has changed the dynamics of what it means to be a mainstream Democrat. It is to Biden's credit, and Warren's, that the Democratic Party is returning to its Roosevelt roots. Those who have pressed from further left, notably Bernie Sanders and Alexandria Ocasio-Cortez, also deserve great credit for pushing outward the boundaries of the possible and for their loyalty to Biden as he has reciprocated.

Others in the world of progressive thinkers and strategists, who have been laboring in the political wilderness for decades, have influenced my thinking, and I hope vice versa. They, along with me, have lived to see their work vindicated.

The list begins with the Economic Policy Institute and Public Citizen, and key leaders of both, notably Thea Lee, Jeff Faux, Larry Mishel, and Heidi Shierholz at EPI; and Sid Wolfe, Rob Weissman, and Lori Wallach at Public Citizen. Among newer think tanks and advocacy groups, three that have made a huge difference include the Open Markets Institute and its leader Barry Lynn; Better Markets and its president Dennis Kelleher;

and the Coalition for a Prosperous America, led by Michael Stumo. Other valued friends and colleagues in the world of advocacy research are Sabeel Rahman (now in the administration), Heather McGhee, Felicia Wong, Todd Tucker, and Teresa Ghilarducci.

I count all of these good people as teachers and friends, as well as co-conspirators. Their combined budgets equal what a middling hedge fund takes in maybe in a week. The fact that they have fought predatory capitalism almost to a draw, and have become the collective extramural thank tank of the Biden administration, is a testament to the power of ideas and of personal conscience over sheer wealth.

My friends and colleagues in the labor movement have been longtime sources of strategic insight—especially the late Rich Trumka, Damon Silvers, Mike Podhorzer, Mary Kay Henry, and Randi Weingarten, among many others. Among those who write about labor, I am grateful for my friendship with Steve Greenhouse, Nelson Lichtenstein, and Katherine V. Stone.

I appreciate the wisdom and dedication of organizers who have helped enrich my thinking, including Heather Booth and her late husband Paul, Dan Cantor, Brian Kettenring, Deepak Bhargava, Steven Lerner, Steve Rosenthal, Chuck Collins, Marshall Ganz, Lindsay Zafir, Ernesto Cortes, George Goehl, and Michael Ansara.

I have also benefited from ongoing conversations with colleagues and friends committed to defending and extending political, racial, and economic democracy, notably Miles Rapoport, Ian Bassin, Randall Kennedy, Liza Goitein, Jane Mansbridge, Theda Skocpol, Nan Aron, Richard Rothstein, Todd Gitlin, Lee Webb, Bob Ross, Dick Flacks, Ganesh Sitaraman, Peter Barnes, Richard McGahey, Robert Pollin, David Harris, David Howell, Richard Parker, Jacob Hacker, Richard Valelly, Stan Greenberg, and Reuven Avi-Yonah.

In my work on industrial policy and China policy, I have gained insights from the brave band of early dissenters whose warnings have been confirmed, especially Clyde Prestowitz, James Mann, Mike Wessel, Scott Paul, Pat Mulloy, Philip Singerman, Rush Doshi, and Robert Lighthizer.

Among Roosevelt historians, I have benefited from those whose work I've read with appreciation, including Jefferson Cowie and Eric Rauchway, and those I've been fortunate to also know personally, notably Doris Kearns Goodwin, Michael Hiltzik, and William Leuchtenburg.

One other intellectual connection that has informed my thinking is my affiliation with research networks who work in the spirit of Karl Polanyi. Thanks to Margie Mendell, Kari Polanyi Levitt, and Andreas Novy, among many others.

At the *American Prospect*, now in its thirty-third year, my colleagues have been a continuing source of political insight and wisdom as well as editorial guidance. Special thanks to David Dayen, Harold Meyerson, Gabrielle Gurley, Jonathan Guyer, Susanna Beiser, Anna Graizbord, and to Amy Hanauer, Mike Stern, Derrick Jackson, and Paul Starr. Some of the issues in this book have been treated in my *Prospect* articles. Thanks also to the other editors who have published my work on some of these themes, especially Emily Greenhouse at the *New York Review of Books*.

At Brandeis, my faculty colleagues and students live the connection between policy, politics, and social justice. I am indebted to David Weil, Lisa Lynch, and Mike Doonan, among many others, and to my students. So many of my ideas are enriched by class discussions.

A thank you to Joe Stiglitz and his wife and intellectual partner Anya Schiffrin, for a lifetime of prescient insights and practical contributions at the intersection of capitalism, globalism, and democracy. Special thanks to Joe for writing a generous foreword to this book.

I appreciate the professionalism and enthusiasm of the people at The New Press, Marc Favreau and Emily Albarillo, and thanks to my skilled copy editor, Brian Baughan, and to my agent, Sydelle Kramer.

I've lost count of how many books my wife, Joan Fitzgerald, has reviewed and improved, reading every line of every draft. I reciprocate by closely reading her work. It is one small part of a splendid alliance. If I am good at explaining things in print, I owe a lot of that to Joan. And so much more.

Notes

Foreword

xi **"enlightenment advances"**: These ideas are set out more fully in my books *People, Power, and Profits: Progressive Capitalism for an Age of Discontent* (New York: W.W. Norton, 2019), published in paperback in 2020, and in *Creating a Learning Society: A New Approach to Growth, Development, and Social Progress*, with Bruce C. Greenwald (New York: Columbia University Press, 2014). Reader's Edition published 2015.

xiv **reshaping the economy**: These ideas are elaborated in D.D. Gatti, M. Gallegati, B. Greenwald, A. Russo, and J.E. Stiglitz, "Mobility Constraints, Productivity Trends, and Extended Crises," *Journal of Economic Behavior & Organization* 83, no. 3 (2012): 375–93. A more accessible rendition is in Joseph E. Stiglitz, "The Book of Jobs," *Vanity Fair*, January 2012, reprinted in *The Great Divide: Unequal Societies and What We Can Do About Them* (New York: W.W. Norton, 2015). Published in paperback in 2016.

xv **exactly the opposite direction**: Critical contributions were provided by Kenneth Arrow and Gerard Debreu, who showed that markets were efficient only under highly restrictive conditions. Bruce Greenwald and I carried the analysis further, showing essentially that whenever information was imperfect or markets incomplete—that is, always—markets were not efficient. Arrow, Debreu, and I all received Nobel prizes for our work. See K.J. Arrow, "An Extension of the Basic Theorems of Classical Welfare Economics," in *Proceedings of the Second Berkeley Symposium on Mathematical Statistics and Probability*, ed. Jerzy Neyman (Berkeley: University of California Press, 1951), 507–32; Gerard Debreu, *The Theory of Value: An Axiomatic Analysis of Economic Equilibrium* (New Haven, CT: Yale University Press, 1959); and B.C. Greenwald and J.E. Stiglitz, "Externalities in Economies with Imperfect Information and Incomplete Markets," *Quarterly Journal of Economics* 101, no. 2 (1986): 229–64.

xv **his ideological stance**: See, for instance, S.J. Grossman and J.E. Stiglitz, "On Value Maximization and Alternative Objectives of the Firm," *Journal of Finance* 32, no. 2 (1977): 389–402.

Chapter 1: The Improbable Progressive

6 **Even the *New York Times*:** "Democrats, Get Real," *New York Times*, November 4, 2021.

7 **original ten-year infrastructure plan:** Aatish Bhatia and Quoctrung Bui, "The Infrastructure Plan: What's In and What's Out," *New York Times*, updated August 10, 2021, https://www.nytimes.com/interactive/2021/07/28/up shot/infrastructure-breakdown.html.

19 **lengthy investigative feature:** Robert Kuttner, "Falling Upward: The Surprising Survival of Larry Summers," *American Prospect*, July 13, 2020.

21 **a bitterly ironic poem:** Brecht, "Die Lösung":

> After the uprising of the 17th June
> The Secretary of the Writers Union
> Had leaflets distributed in the Stalinallee
> Stating that the people
> Had forfeited the confidence of the government
> And could win it back only
> By redoubled efforts. Would it not be easier
> In that case for the government
> To dissolve the people
> And elect another?

23 **a famous argument:** Michał Kalecki, "Political Aspects of Full Employment," *Political Quarterly* 14, no. 4 (1943): 322–30, https://pluto.mscc.huji .ac.il/~mshalev/ppe/Kalecki_FullEmployment.pdf.

Chapter 2: Roosevelt's Fragile Revolution

27 **"I want to tell you what has been done":** "March 12, 1933: Fireside Chat 1: On the Banking Crisis," Miller Center, University of Virginia, https://millercenter.org/the-presidency/presidential-speeches/march-12-1933 -fireside-chat-1-banking-crisis.

29 **some four thousand banks failed:** Michael Hilzik, *The New Deal: A Modern History* (New York: Free Press, 2011), 94.

30 **New Deal was a temporary great exception:** Jefferson Cowie, *The Great Exception: The New Deal & the Limits of American Politics* (Princeton, NJ: Princeton University Press, 2017).

30 **As late as 1940:** Robert A. Margo, "Employment and Unemployment in the 1930s," *Journal of Economic Perspectives* 7, no. 2 (1993), https://fraser.stlouis fed.org/files/docs/meltzer/maremp 93.pdf.

33 **"If enacted, it would"**: Joel Seligman, *The Transformation of Wall Street: A History of the Securities and Exchange Commission and Modern Corporate Finance* (New York: Aspen Publishers, 2003), 85–86.

35 **"The New Deal matters"**: Eric Rauchway, *Why the New Deal Matters* (New Haven, CT: Yale University Press, 2001), 7.

39 **"At the 1932 Democratic Convention"**: William Leuchtenburg, *The White House Looks South: Franklin D. Roosevelt, Harry S. Truman, Lyndon B. Johnson* (Baton Rouge, LA: LSU Press), 39.

41 **many Northern politicians wanted segregated public housing**: Interview with Richard Rothstein.

42 **"If a neighborhood is to retain stability"**: Rothstein, *The Color of Law: A Forgotten History of How Our Government Segregated America* (New York: Liveright, 2019), 65.

42 **the case of a white San Francisco schoolteacher**: Rothstein, *Color of Law*, 67.

43 **"I had no sooner taken my seat"**: Leuchtenburg, *White House Looks South*, 123.

44 **"Ed Smith voted for a bill"**: Leuchtenburg, *White House Looks South,* 98.

46 **Huff spent five days in jail:** Thomas Borstelmann, *The Cold War and the Color Line: American Race Relations in the Global Arena* (Cambridge, MA: Harvard University Press, 2001), 32.

Chapter 3: The New Deal's Long Half-Life

49 **"repression of finance"**: Carmen Reinhart and M. Belen Sbrancia, *The Liquidation of Government Debt* (Washington, DC: International Monetary Fund, 2015). See also Carmen Reinhart and Kenneth Rogoff, *Sovereign Debt Crises: Lessons Learned and Lessons Forgotten* (Washington, DC: International Monetary Fund, 2013).

50 **"the euthanasia of the *rentier*"**: John Maynard Keynes, *The General Theory of Employment, Interest, and Money* (London: Macmillan, 1936), 345.

53 **"Harry, this is the first time"**: Leuchtenburg, *White House Looks South*, 149–50.

54 **"look up that damn nigger preacher"**: David McCullough, *Truman* (New York: Simon and Schuster, 2003), 683.

56 **"We cannot recall"**: Leuchtenburg, *White House Looks South*, 172.

57 **"it is not Russia"**: Borstelmann, *Cold War and the Color Line*, 77.

58 **"the cheering and stomping"**: McCullough, *Truman*, 360.

59 **"It was to underscore ideological differences"**: Alonzo Hamby, *Man of the People: A Life of Harry S. Truman* (Oxford: Oxford University Press, 1995), 433.

60 **"These Republican gluttons of privilege"**: McCullough, *Truman*, 800.

60 **"Our primary concern"**: McCullough, *Truman*, 802.

65 **"Carry out your agreements"**: Harry S. Truman, *Memoirs*, vol. I, *Year of Decisions* (New York: Doubleday and Company, 1955), 401.

67 **contemplating a U.S. exit:** See discussion in David Halberstam, *The Best and the Brightest* (New York: Random House, 1972).

Chapter 4: LBJ's Tragedy and Ours

70 **"I never thought then"**: Lyndon Johnson, Address to Congress, March 15, 1965, http://www.lbjlibrary.org/lyndon-baines-johnson/speeches-films/president-johnsons-special-message-to-the-congress-the-american-promise.

72 "**But it's going to cost you"**: Nick Kotz, *Judgment Days: Lyndon Baines Johnson, Martin Luther King, Jr., and the Laws That Changed America* (Boston: Houghton Mifflin, 2005), 38.

72 **"The so-called civil rights program"**: Merle Miller, *Lyndon: An Oral Biography* (New York: G.P. Putnam's Sons, 1980) 18.

73 **"The Negro today asks justice"**: Kotz, *Judgment Days*, 61.

73 **"I'm going to pass the Civil Rights Act"**: Kotz, *Judgment Days*, 16.

74 **"I'll have to have you-all's help"**: Kotz, *Judgment Days*, 19.

75 **"He's a turncoat"**: Leuchtenburg, *White House Looks South*, 330.

76 **"It was a segregationist's worst nightmare"**: Ari Berman, *Give Us the Ballot: The Modern Struggle for Voting Rights in America* (New York: Farrar, Straus and Giroux, 2015,) 42.

77 **"I was still illegitimate"**: Doris Kearns Goodwin, *Lyndon Johnson and the American Dream* (New York: Harper Collins, 1976), 170.

78 **"had run for sheriff once"**: Halberstam, *The Best and the Brightest*, 41.

79 **"whip hell out of some Communists"**: Kotz, *Judgment Days*, 21.

81 **"taking the communist line"**: Halberstam, *The Best and the Brightest*, 254.

84 **the Second Reconstruction was sticking:** Richard M. Valelly, *The Two Reconstructions: The Struggle for Black Enfranchisement* (Chicago: University of Chicago Press, 2004).

85 *The Triumph of Voting Rights in the South*: Charles S. Bullock III and Ronald Keith Gaddie, *The Triumph of Voting Rights in the South* (Norman: University of Oklahoma Press, 2009).

88 **had introduced new voting restrictions:** Carol Anderson, *One Person, No Vote: How Voter Suppression Is Destroying Our Democracy* (New York: Bloomsbury Publishing, 2018), 72.

Chapter 5: The Great Reversal

90 **the divergence keeps growing wider:** "The Productivity–Pay Gap," Economic Policy Institute, https://www.epi.org/productivity-pay-gap.

The Growing Gap Between Productivity and Pay

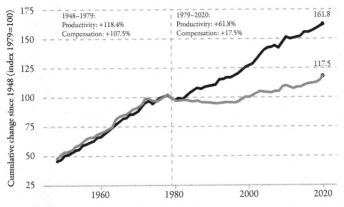

1948–1979:
Productivity: +118.4%
Compensation: +107.5%

1979–2020:
Productivity: +61.8%
Compensation: +17.5%

161.8

117.5

Data are for compensation (wages and benefits) of production/nonsupervisory workers in the private sector and net productivity of the total economy. "Net productivity" is the growth of output of goods and services less depreciation per hour worked.

Source: EPI analysis of unpublished Total Economy Productivity data from Bureau of Labor Statistics (BLS) Labor Productivity and Costs program, wage data from the BLS Current Employment Statistics, BLS Employment Cost Trends, BLS Consumer Price Index, and Bureau of Economic Analysis National Income and Product Accounts.

91 **a less egalitarian income distribution:** See Robert Kuttner, "The Declining Middle," *Atlantic Monthly*, July 1983.

96 **"Government cannot solve our problems":** President Jimmy Carter, "The State of the Union Address Delivered Before a Joint Session of the Congress,"

January 19, 1978, https://www.presidency.ucsb.edu/documents/the-state-the-union -address-delivered-before-joint-session-the-congress-1.

96 **"we still would be in the Great Depression"**: Arthur Schlesinger Jr., "The Great Carter Mystery," *New Republic*, April 12, 1980, https://newrepublic .com/article/104365/the-great-carter-mystery.

96 **"a whole host of special one-shot factors"**: Alan Blinder, *The Anatomy of Double-Digit Inflation the 1970s*, NBER, 1982, https://www.nber.org/system /files/chapters/c11462/c11462.pdf.

98 **proposed just such a freeze**: John Kenneth Galbraith, "Professor Galbraith Reluctantly Recommends Wage-Price Controls—the Cure for Runaway Inflation," *New York Times*, June 7, 1970.

98 **dampen inflationary expectations**: Robert F. Lanzilotti et al., *Phase II in Review: The Price Commission Experience* (Washington, DC: Brookings Institution, 1975).

98 **"I do not believe in wage and price controls"**: Jeff Faux, *The Servant Economy: Where America's Elite Is Sending the Middle Class* (New York: John Wiley, 2012), 60.

104 **"It's too easy to game"**: Claudia H. Deutsch, "An Early Advocate of Stock Options Debunks Himself," *New York Times*, April 3, 2005.

106 **fell faster before deregulation**: Robert Kuttner, *Everything for Sale: The Virtues and Limits of Markets* (New York: Alfred A. Knopf, 1996), 258.

Chapter 6: Bad Economics, Worse Politics

112 **"I heard you"**: "Transcript of Mondale Address Accepting Party Nomination," *New York Times*, July 20, 1984.

115 **logic of "rent seeking"**: James Buchanan and Gordon Tulloch, *The Calculus of Consent* (Ann Arbor: University of Michigan Press, 1962).

124 **"I think you'll be president one day"**: Al From, "Recruiting Bill Clinton," *The Atlantic*, December 3, 2013.

125 **"associate liberalism with tax and spending"**: William Galston and Elaine Ciulla Kamarck, "The Politics of Evasion: Democrats and the Presidency," Progressive Policy Institute, September 1989, https://www.progressivepolicy .org/wp-content/uploads/2013/03/Politics_of_Evasion.pdf.

127 **"the first generation of Americans"**: Theodore White, "The Shaping of the Presidency, 1984," *Time* magazine, November 19, 1984, p. 38, http://content .time.com/time/subscriber/article/0,33009,950195,00.html.

130 **"R&D, technology, infrastructure and education":** Stiglitz, *The Roaring Nineties: A New History of the World's Most Prosperous Decade* (New York: W.W. Norton,) 52–53.

130 **The deficit was cut:** Kimberly Amadeo, "US Budget Deficit by Year Compared to GDP, Debt Increase, and Events," The Balance, https://www.thebalance.com/us-deficit-by-year-3306306.

130 **was precisely what it had been:** "30 Year Treasury Rate—39 Year Historical Chart," Macrotrends, https://www.macrotrends.net/2521/30-year-treasury-bond-rate-yield-chart.

131 **"privatized Keynesianism":** Colin Crouch, *The Strange Non-death of Neoliberalism* (Cambridge: Polity Press, 2011).

132 **stock market bubble added $5 trillion:** Robert Kuttner, *The Squandering of America: How the Failure of Our Politics Undermines Our Prosperity* (New York: Alfred A. Knopf, 2007), 166–67.

Chapter 7: Obama's Missed Moment

137 **"market that favors Wall Street over Main Street":** "Transcript: Obama on 'Renewing the American Economy,'" *New York Times*, March 27, 2008, https://www.nytimes.com/2008/03/27/us/politics/27text-obama.html.

141 **"the worst financial crisis since World War II":** Simon Johnson and James Kwak, *13 Bankers: The Wall Street Takeover and the Next Financial Meltdown* (New York: Random House, 2010), 9.

144 **"Wall Street was in the room":** Interview with Jeff Faux.

151 **standard private equity strategy:** Atul Gupta et al., "Does Private Equity Investment in Healthcare Benefit Patients? Evidence from Nursing Homes," National Bureau of Economic Research, NBER Working Paper Series, February 2021, https://www.nber.org/system/files/working_papers/w28474/w28474.pdf.

151 **the wreckage of local newspapers:** David Bauder and David A. Lieb, "More Than 1,400 Cities and Towns in U.S. Have Lost Newspapers in Past 15 Years," *South Bend Tribune*, March 11, 2019.

152 **contributed two books of my own:** *The Squandering of America* (2007) and *A Presidency in Peril: The Inside Story of Obama's Promise, Wall Street's Power, and the Struggle to Control Our Economic Future* (White River Junction, VT: Chelsea Green, 2010).

157 **put into a government receivership:** Reed Hundt, *A Crisis Wasted: Barack Obama's Defining Decisions* (New York: Simon and Schuster, 2019), 235.

157 **"it was like a punch in the gut"**: Sheila Bair, *Bull by the Horns: Fighting to Save Main Street from Wall Street and Wall Street from Itself* (New York: Simon and Schuster, 2012), 142.

161 **"'That would be good for the banks'"**: Hundt, *Crisis Wasted*, 133.

Chapter 8: America's Last Chance

168 **Voters under thirty broke:** Ruth Igielnik, Scott Keeter, and Hannah Hartig, "Behind Biden's 2020 Victory," June 30, 2021, Pew Research Center, https://www.pewresearch.org/politics/2021/06/30/behind-bidens-2020-victory.

168 **Fear of Trump helped Biden:** Yair Ghitza and Jonathan Robinson, "WhatHappened in 2020," Catalist, https://catalist.us/wh-national/?link_id =2&can_id=58bb91bd27f3a462663108174dfb602a.

172 **"handing Democrats a political grenade":** "Texas's Abortion Law Blunder," editorial, *Wall Street Journal*, September 2, 2021.

175 **most impressive economic planning document:** The White House, *Building Resilient Supply Chains, Revitalizing American Manufacturing, and Fostering Broad-Based Growth: 100-Day Reviews Under Executive Order 14017*, June 2021, Washington, DC, https://www.whitehouse.gov/wp-content/up loads/2021/06/100-day-supply-chain-review-report.pdf.

177 **the order Biden issued:** "Executive Order on Promoting Competition in the American Economy," White House Briefing Room, July 9, 2021, https://www.whitehouse.gov/briefing-room/presidential-actions/2021/07/09 /executive-order-on-promoting-competition-in-the-american-economy.

178 **existing antitrust law could be applied:** Lina M. Khan, "Amazon's Antitrust Paradox," *Yale Law Journal* 126, no. 3 (2017), https://www.yalelawjournal .org/note/amazons-antitrust-paradox.

179 **"right of every businessman":** The White House, "Remarks by President Biden at Signing of an Executive Order Promoting Competition in the American Economy," July 9, 2021, https://www.whitehouse.gov/briefing-room/speeches-re marks/2021/07/09/remarks-by-president-biden-at-signing-of-an-executive-order -promoting-competition-in-the-american-economy.

181 **"global systemically important banks":** Frank Partnoy, "The Looming Bank Collapse," *The Atlantic*, July/August 2020.

185 **ultra-high-speed internet package:** EPB, https://epb.com.

187 **revive socially owned housing:** See Ganesh Sitaraman and Anne L. Alstott, *The Public Option: How to Expand Freedom, Increase Opportunity, and Promote Equality* (Cambridge, MA: Harvard University Press, 2019).

187 **system for early childhood education:** U.S. Department of Defense, *Report to the Congressional Defense Committees on Department of Defense Child Development Programs*, 2020, https://securefamiliesinitiative.org/wp-content/up loads/2021/04/Report-on-DoD-Child-Development-Programs-June-2020.pdf.

188 **"blame new immigrants or people of color":** Ian Haney López, *Merge Left: Fusing Race and Class, Winning Elections, and Saving America* (New York, The New Press, 2019), 175–76.

189 **the South shortchanged ordinary whites:** Heather McGhee, *The Sum of Us: What Racism Costs Everyone and How We Can Prosper Together* (New York: One World, 2021), 19–20.

193 **went heavily for Biden:** Ruth Igielnik, Scott Keeter and Hannah Hartig, "Behind Biden's 2020 Victory," Pew Research Center, June 30, 2021, https://www .pewresearch.org/politics/2021/06/30/behind-bidens-2020-victory.

Index

About the Author

Robert Kuttner is co-founder and co-editor of the *American Prospect*. He holds the Ida and Meyer Kirstein Chair at Brandeis University, and is the author of twelve previous books. He was a founder of the Economic Policy Institute and is a former columnist for *BusinessWeek* and the *Boston Globe*.

His other positions have included national staff writer on the *Washington Post*, economics editor of the *New Republic*, and chief investigator of the U.S. Senate Banking Committee. He was educated at Oberlin, the University of California, and the London School of Economics. He holds honorary doctorates from Oberlin and Swarthmore. He lives in Boston.

Publishing in the Public Interest

Thank you for reading this book published by The New Press. The New Press is a nonprofit, public interest publisher. New Press books and authors play a crucial role in sparking conversations about the key political and social issues of our day.

We hope you enjoyed this book and that you will stay in touch with The New Press. Here are a few ways to stay up to date with our books, events, and the issues we cover:

- Sign up at www.thenewpress.com/subscribe to receive updates on New Press authors and issues and to be notified about local events
- www.facebook.com/newpressbooks
- www.twitter.com/thenewpress
- www.instagram.com/thenewpress

Please consider buying New Press books for yourself; for friends and family; or to donate to schools, libraries, community centers, prison libraries, and other organizations involved with the issues our authors write about.

The New Press is a 501(c)(3) nonprofit organization. You can also support our work with a tax-deductible gift by visiting www.thenewpress.com/donate.